THROUGH THE FIRE

THE JONATHAN STREET STORY

Garrath Rosslee
with Jonathan Street

© 2021

Sarah, Candice …
It is said that "when the student is ready,
the teacher(s) arrive."

Thank you both for so much.
G

Forward

When a man by the name of Jonathan Street, reached out to me from prison with a simple and handwritten poem, I was afraid. My strong-minded niece was in love, she had told me, and they planned to marry when he was released on parole. Suddenly the reality was too close and the implications too frightening to contemplate. But here I am, at the request of Jonathan, writing a forward for this remarkable and painful story of change and his path to a new life.

As a then Registered Psychotherapist, in practice in Canada, the months and years following the poem event was a time to reflect with family and confront my own deepest values and beliefs empowering transformation in the lives of my patients. Ultimately it was not unreasonable to conclude .... "Why not Jonathan Street?"

The reading and rereading of the transcript and following its transformation into this book has been a privilege. The Jonathan Street story is skillfully narrated by Psychologist, Dr Garrath Rosslee, based on numerous interviews with Jonathan, his family and friends and my family. One cannot but notice that the account is deeply personal to Garrath who not only shares his relationship and experience with change in his work but in his personal life. His insights, observations and his research-based interpretations validate how when embracing the challenges of change, as in Jonathan's case, transformation can be a powerful outcome. The book has emerged from its conceptual goal as a story of transformation for Jonathan and Garrath to one that offers hope to each and all of us engaged in this particularly challenging process.

"Through the Fire" explores the impact of choice as Jonathan struggles to find his way, it follows the changes to his philosophy of life, the fulfilment of his emerging and deepest need for reparation and his "walking through the fire" of transformation. The story tells of his maturing and developing a sure foundation of role models, beliefs and love evidenced in the now by his release from prison, his active involvement in productive employment, his marriage to Chrissie, and the birth of their baby girl.

His story begins with all the stark reality of his ego driven actions, his anxieties, his need to belong behaviours and ultimately his crimes with the sad inevitability of outcomes. It tells of his incarceration. It shares the heartbreak of loss and the inspiration of realizations. It speaks to the qualities of conscious decision making, balance and cultivating resilience. And it tells of the power of love and belief of not only Chrissie, who in her own journey faithfully supported her man, but the families and friends who advised him, and believed in him, at times with despair, but with hope and faith.

Transformation is an ongoing process and requires self awareness, effort and focus, Jonathan told me recently. We discover in the final chapters how change is time directed and earned, and redefined as an emotional task driven by the belief of possibility. I quote Garraths findings "Adult transformation is primarily an emotional process. The building blocks of adult transformation are purpose, self-awareness, daily action, and hope. Change enables us to find freedom in confinement" (p.82).

However, important questions came to mind as the book draws to a close. I felt an urgency for these to be addressed. And phrases like "adequate time served", "moral justification", "recidivism rates of up to 95%"," sustainability of long-term change" loomed, not to be ignored. It was as if Garrath had read my mind as the next pages revealed his insightful and candid answers.

And finally, may I add that the essence of change as an active potential resonates as these two men, Garrath and Jonathan, embrace with awe and respectful self examination the "transformative year of the book" in the final pages. This book is as emotive as it is eminently readable.

Thank you both for the opportunity and honour to offer comment and observation on this remarkable endeavour.

Elizabeth Human
M. Rad (T) UP: MACP Canada
Master of Arts Counselling Psychology

Index

Part 1: **FUCK IT**

Part 2: **INCARCERATION**

Part 3: **RESPITE**

Part 4: **REDEMPTION**

Part 1:

"FUCK IT"

I
2020

The first thing I noticed about Jonathan Street was the way he moved: a slow, measured stride. He was shorter than I had imagined, and stockier. Being the son of a hairdresser, I couldn't miss his near-flawless hair: combed and creamed to perfection. He was neatly dressed in black jeans, his brand new white sneakers matching his fitted white T-shirt. He greeted me with a broad smile and a firm handshake, and I was struck by a gentleness about his manner. This was not the tattooed brute of an ex-con I had imagined.

A week earlier, in the height of the Covid-19 pandemic under lockdown restrictions, I'd been distributing copies of my first two books at a good friend's business premises on the eastern side of Johannesburg. I came across a friendly, chatty blonde who eyed my books and asked, "Are you a writer?"

"I am," I replied. "It's become a bit of a midlife hobby. I enjoy it."

"What do you write about?"

"I don't do fiction - I'm not that talented or creative. My first three works are non-fiction, about things that interest me. But I hope they're useful and practical for readers, too. I'm Garrath, by the way."

The blonde told me her name was Chrissie and asked me to tell her more about my books.

"Well, it's important to me that my writing is about something constructive," I told her. "And that it's helpful to the community. I'm an organisational change specialist, you see. I aim to write stuff that carries a positive message, stuff that will facilitate change, but be entertaining too."

Chrissie flashed a disarming smile. "Have I got a story for you!" she said.

"Oh, ja?" I wasn't sure where this was going, but I took the bait. "What is it?"

"It's about my husband. He's just been released after thirteen years in prison."

"Sheesh, that's a long time. What was he in for?"

"He got into a fight and one of the guys lost his life, so he left the country. When he came back, he was involved in another incident..."

I didn't need Chrissie to finish the story. "That's Jonathan Street!" I exclaimed.

"How in heaven's name did you know that?"

Jonathan Street's story had captured my imagination from the moment I first read his name in a news report about a violent fight that broke out at a well-known eatery near Kyalami in the northern suburbs of Johannesburg. At the time, I worked not far from the place, and my then-girlfriend and I often met there after work to avoid an hour of sitting in traffic to get home.

Many people complain about Johannesburg being a dirty, overcrowded and polluted city, which it probably is in some parts. In other spots, its sunrises and sunsets are as splendid as anywhere. The grill was a convenient, wholesome, relaxed place to unwind and enjoy dinner outside and as the sun set.

That this familiar place had been the scene of a conflict which resulted in death for one young man and life on the run for others was discomforting.

I had followed the case closely, my main source of information being radio and newspaper reports. The media reported on the case in a frenzy of sensationalism, with frequent headlines about the 'ex-bouncer', the 'bouncing mafia', and top cops threatening that 'heads will roll'.

As popular interest in the proceedings faded, I relied on the Mail & Guardian for updates. The reporting was detailed, balanced and thorough, and I remember being struck by the fact that this youngster grew up just a few blocks from my home, that he went to the same school my cousin had been headboy of, that he had worked as a bouncer at places I occasionally partied at. I felt as if I knew him.

I read he'd gone abroad on the run, and I was intrigued: How did this young man with a seemingly normal upbringing find himself in such deep trouble with the law and no real prospect of a future?

Later, I read that he'd returned to South Africa, only to be embroiled in another tragedy at a strip-joint in the east of Johannesburg, not far from where I lived. Whenever I found myself driving through the main drag of 'The Vale', as it was known, I'd pass the scene of the incident and mull over what

3

had actually happened that fateful night all those years ago. Another young life lost, another family scarred forever. The Jonathan Street saga, it seemed, continued.

I'm a psychologist trained in systems and process psychology, so I can't help analysing behaviour: following the trail of actions and episodes to see how they may generate a pattern. Talking to Chrissie so many years later, I was surprised by what I could recall of the story. I remembered the case in fine detail, remembered how it had gripped me. The tragedy of the turn of events had really made an impression on me, and I remembered how I'd felt a sadness for the lost lives, the destroyed families. And I'd often wondered how it had all begun.

Jonathan, Chrissie told me, had undergone a major, self-directed reformation in prison. He finished school and went on to complete an N6 in Human Resources Management. He'd continued training and stayed in shape. He'd taken up Bible studies, studied theology, and became a churchgoer. He took part in drama groups and gave talks on the dangers of drug abuse.

And he'd found the love of his life.

Chrissie's narrative left me filled with hope and the possibility of renewal - a welcome and refreshing change, following as it did on my recent return from a six-month project in the jungles of Africa, landing smack-bang in the middle of lockdown. Feeling the loss of personal freedoms and struggling with the sense of confinement, little did I know that I'd learn much more about the loss of freedom in the months to come. One of my partners talks incessantly about synchronicity, and I thought of this often as the work progressed.

Adult change has formed a major part of my career. I have had the good fortune of working with global businesses, African-centric operations, and many commercial enterprises and NGOs. My work has been kind to me, taking me to the Americas, Europe, Middle East and Africa. I have, in the last 25-odd years, had many opportunities to observe adults grappling with personal and organisational change. I have experienced change first-hand, too: starting a business, having a family, divorce, changing homes, work uncertainty, and the numerous challenges of adult transitions.

Jonathan's story of personal transformation resonated with me.

I had arrived early at our rendezvous and positioned myself opposite a window so as to observe Jonathan and Chrissie arriving – a seat that was also close to the door, lest a hasty exit was required. From my vantage point, I watched husband and wife emerge from their car and approach the entrance, chatting comfortably with each other. They could have been talking about the weather or office life; an average couple on an average Saturday morning.

Jonathan said little during the course of our first meeting. I had introduced myself and shared what I do, and he seemed interested in psychology and my experience of working in different countries. He shared with me that he studied humanities in the workplace, perhaps a search for common ground between us.

It wasn't long before Jonathan got down to the purpose of the meeting.

"Why would you want to write my story?"

"If I understand correctly," I told him. "Your narrative is one of redemption, of personal change, and all the difficulties and challenges that go along with it. That's my thing. That's what I spend my days thinking about. That's the stuff that gets me excited." This seemed to make sense to Jonathan. He nodded and seemed to be chewing it over in his mind.

"And why would people read it?"

"Look, I don't want to write a crime exposé or investigative piece. I'm no Mandy Weiner. The thing about your story that hooked me, the thing I think people will want to read about, is that it's a real good-news story. I want to write about the potential for change in everyone."

Jonathan's face lit up at this. He nodded again. After a moment he said quietly, "Deal done," and smiled gently at me.

II
IN THE BEGINNING

In preliminary meetings, Jonathan and I explored the structure of the book, it's primary, secondary and tertiary strains. We discussed the logistics of sharing information, the tone, the style, the timelines.

A necessary conversation we had early on was how the process of writing Jonathan's story could elicit and re-ignite painful feelings from the past that he would be forced to confront. Demons he may have thought were dead buried could be resurrected, he may be obliged to hear other people's versions of the stories that made up his past.

We talked a bit about the fact that, while this is his story, others' experiences of the events would be laid bare, and their versions of his stories may not align with his. I advised Jonathan to be prepared for any eventuality, to treat everything he hears as input for his personal development.

During this early stage of our planning, we agreed that this was not going to be a lurid, tell-all tale. Neither of us wanted to produce a sensational work, going into detail about the events, names, actions and episodes of Jonathan's life. In order to steer clear of verging into tabloid territory, we agreed that just three names would be disclosed: Jonathan's, Chrissie's and mine.

I spent some time developing a protocol to guide my research interviews with Jonathan's friends and family, and work on the book began in earnest as winter descended over Joburg in lockdown.

In no time, our "Saturday Sessions" settled into a predictable pattern and became a fixture in both our lives: Jonathan's parole conditions permitted travel and visitation between midday and 6 pm, so we'd try to get two visits to friends and family into each session, but time was tight.

We'd start each visit with a cooldrink, and then we'd eat. We always ate. It was as if Jonathan's mates and family were making up for his time in prison, we ate in such volume and variety. I'm certain I put on a few kilograms from all the pastries and pizzas we consumed.

With stomachs full, we'd move onto the interviews. These conversations lasted for about an hour and a half at a time, and interviewees were candid, honest and direct. Jonathan sat in on all of them. I sometimes felt for him, having to hear his loved ones recounting his aggressiveness and his bad-boy ways. No words were minced, either. The people in Jonathan's life were clear about their thoughts and feelings.

It was fascinating to engage with people who were familiar with both the 'old' and the 'new' Jonathan, but I often wondered if being in the homes of friends was challenging for Jonathan. Fourteen years had passed since he'd been locked up, and his peers had all progressed in their lives: settled down, started families. We'd visit them in their homes, where the average luxuries of regular suburban lives were in evidence, while Jonathan seemed to have so little. There were moments when I sensed Jonathan's regret at having lost a decade and a half of his life, but more often than not, he exhibited gratitude for having a second chance, appreciation for what little he has. I found his outlook remarkable.

Before long, a picture began to emerge.

Jonathan, his mother told me on the phone, was a kind, lovable and generous child. He would often bring her a flower picked from the garden, handing it to her with a kiss on her cheek, saying, "Mom, I love you." He battled with seizures, which were eventually brought under control. "But he would drive us crazy!" she said. "He wouldn't sleep, and he was an extremely busy child."

With time, it seems, Jonathan outgrew his busyness and sleeplessness. But while he was in primary school, he began to show worrying signs of aggression: fighting with his peers, burning locusts and chasing chickens. Friends and neighbours began to complain about his behaviour. Jonathan's parents attempted to manage his behaviour, but no intervention seemed to work.

In high school, Jonathan's mom continued, the trouble escalated, as did Jonathan's aggressive behaviour. He was frequently involved in fights.

Jonathan had confided in me on a separate occasion that he'd been bullied in high school. It was at some point during this time Jonathan's mother was describing that Jonathan started boxing with a friend. It was an attempt on his part to develop fighting skills, perhaps with the intention of standing up for himself. The kids who were bullying him, though, seemed to consider this development a problem. "They thought I was trying to be a 'breeker,'" Jonathan had told me, using the colloquial term for a tough guy.

There was a man that lived down the road from Jonathan's family who befriended Jonathan. "He was a good influence," Jonathan says. "A good boxer, a strong man. He tried to keep me on the right path. He warned me about staying away from the nightclub lifestyle."

Despite this good influence, Jonathan's life was spiralling downwards. His grades dropped. His casual drinking habits became binges. He began experimenting with drugs.

Jonathan's bullies were older than him: matric students and rugby players. In the social hierarchy of South African schools at the time, these were the big deal kids. They were the somebodies - Jonathan felt like a nobody.

In many respects, Jonathan's exploits were an attempt on his part to impress the cool kids, to garner their respect. That they only seemed to increase the bullying caused a great deal of frustration for Jonathan.

I thought of this earlier conversation with Jonathan about bullying as he and I quietly listened to his mother, laughing and crying as she recounted Jonathan's transgressions. She described her own anxieties and fears as a result of Jonathan's behaviour. Looking over at Jonathan, I noticed his face had reddened, he was blinking back tears. I know I was, too.

Towards the end of 2020, as we were wrapping up the first draft of the book, I asked Jonathan whether he could remember a moment in his life, an event, that signalled the start of the tragedy heaped upon tragedy that was to follow. He sent me his reply by voice note.

"It was while I was in high school," he said. "Grade 10. I remember it so well, as if it happened yesterday. It was a grey and dreary day - pretty much how I felt about life at that time. It was break, and I was standing on the school driveway, surrounded by other pupils.

"In a moment, I just... clicked off, like a light. I just switched off and thought, 'Fuck it.' I told myself I didn't give a fuck anymore. Nothing mattered."

III
THE CHALLENGE OF CHANGE

Jonathan and I had been working together on the book for some months when I asked him what, in his 39 years, he had felt most threatened by. Without hesitation, he replied, "The challenge of change."

I wasn't surprised by Jonathan's answer, but it is revealing. Having faced bullying, fist-fights, intimidation by fellow bouncers protecting their territory, life on the run and imprisonment alongside hardened criminals, the thing that Jonathan perceived to be most threatening was change itself: having to shed his old identity and renew himself, to re-evaluate his values and belief system, to actively reshape his attitudes and behaviours.

Change is terrifying. That's why we're so resistant to it.

The theme of change emerged and re-emerged with frequency throughout the process of researching and writing Jonathan's story. Like most adults, Jonathan struggles with deep-seated change.

Meaningful attitudinal and behavioural change, in my experience, is frequently driven by crisis.

Engaging with Jonathan's friends and family provided insight into how Jonathan Street had moved on from the person he was before. It was evident that they had witnessed Jonathan's transformation firsthand.

My observation of Jonathan during the course of our Saturday sessions brought to mind the words of Arnold Mindell, the founder of process oriented psychology: "burning your wood". Burning your wood is a way to increase self-knowledge by grappling with your inner conflicts: identifying your triggers and doing the work to understand them, thereby wresting from them their control over your behaviour. Jonathan was burning his wood: dealing with the consequences of his actions, taking responsibility and confronting himself in order to change.

During the time I worked with Jonathan, visiting his home, meeting his friends and family, I was reminded that change doesn't come easy. Change is an everyday endeavour that requires fortitude, awareness, energy and resilience. Adults, it seems, log into cruise control and change is unlikely unless there is an event of some significance.

That dreary day in 1997, when Jonathan stood on the driveway to school and experienced a mental switch, signalled the start of Jonathan's protracted rebellion. In an instant, Jonathan's respect for anyone and everyone disappeared. He no longer cared. He made a decision to respond to any confrontation with hostility.

At home, Jonathan's disrespect for his parents was in full cry, and his father and mother lived in fear. He recounts that he would take the car from the garage without his parents' permission and do with it as he liked. Jonathan's mom had indicated that this was about the time he started using steroids excessively. At school, he frequently bunked classes and defiantly allowed himself to be seen drinking in his uniform – behaviour that was explicitly forbidden.

"One morning at school," Jonathan says, "I was called to the hall over the intercom."

On arriving, he was met by a group of matrics, who locked the doors to the hall behind him.

"A couple of the guys were interrogating me threateningly." His offence? Wearing earrings after school while in uniform. "I thought it was a bit of a joke," he says. "But then one tried to assault me, and I got scared. I didn't retaliate."

It wasn't long before Jonathan dropped out of school.

After that, his mom told me, Jonathan's life became a gym, drink, drugs, box, eat and sleep routine. He enrolled at a local college, later switching to another, but he admits that drugs, alcohol, clubbing and fighting prevented him from making a success of his studies. When his books were stolen before exams, he responded by getting drunk and getting into another fight. That was the end of his studies.

A friend of Jonathan's helped him get a job as a bouncer at a hotel near his home. He found the work daunting at first, but soon acclimatised to the lifestyle.

"I was on my own power trip," he told me. "Which suited me. Staying at home with my family, not going to school anymore, bouncing at night, going to gym during the day… Doing steroids, drinking excessively. I thought it was pretty cool."

I ask him if he ever thought about the warnings from his friend down the road. "I took no notice," he says.

"I thought he didn't know what he was talking about. I thought I knew better than him."

As we got to know each other better and trust developed, Jonathan began to open up about his bouncing days. After working as a bouncer for a couple of months, he started working for a company that provided security services to nightclubs. Jonathan admired his boss, the business owner. He was a tough man, Jonathan told me, who'd gained his experience working in Hillbrow – the place to be at the time for anyone wanting to make it in the bouncing business. He groomed Jonathan, teaching him things he never knew about fighting – how to maximise the power of his punch, how to handle street situations. "I loved my life," Jonathan says of the time.

Jonathan's mother recalls that period less fondly, saying, "Bouncing became his life." He was still a teen, acting macho and hanging around with men much older than he was who egged him on. Often, she would have to fetch Jonathan after his shift ended, driving to the other side of town at 3 am to meet him outside a club. More than once, she remembers, his shirt was bloodied and torn.

Jonathan's boss became something of a role model for him, and Jonathan began to view the work he was doing as a way to grow his reputation, to become somebody.

"I was very insecure," Jonathan describes himself at the time. "I was always looking for attention, needing to be accepted."

He met many gangsters and men with big reputations, and he enjoyed being around "the guys", despite the fact that - as he often told me directly and indirectly - he was required to prove himself. The values of this set appealed to him: he liked the fighting, the conspicuous money, the flashy cars, clothes and tattoos. Jonathan willingly conformed.

IV
BELONGING

Thinking about Jonathan's troubled early years got me wondering about my own late adolescence. What was important to me then? What drove my anxiety? My own son is nineteen – roughly the age Jonathan was when he encountered this way of life. I chatted informally with him and some of his age mates, and with friends who are parents to kids on the cusp of adulthood. Combining these anecdotal responses with my experiences, I noticed a trend which lead me to clustering my sense of the inner world of late teens according to the following dynamics:

At this stage of life, youngsters seek out a sense of belonging. They value being a part of a group, a team or a subculture.

As they shift away from dependence towards adulthood, late teens seem to have a need for reputation, perhaps seeking out a sense of becoming somebody. This is when many individuals strive for recognition through academics, sport, commerce, technology or a hobby of some kind.

The ego – in the sense of being a vehicle to progress – seems influential at this time, as late adolescents appear to want to feel that they are advancing towards some sort of goal.

Jonathan at nineteen presented these three needs in abundance. And being part of the bouncing fraternity met them.

There's no doubt in my mind that the world of nightclub security ticks all the boxes of a subculture, and I learnt from Jonathan that being a part of this subculture is all about reputation. The anger, aggressiveness and hostility that characterises the bouncing underworld fed Jonathan's ego, and drove him to direct his energies towards making a name for himself in the scene.

Jonathan's appearance was extremely important to him, and he loved the paraphernalia that defined the clique he moved in: the expensive trainers, the bling, the tattoos.

"My tattoos brought me joy," he tells me so many years later, displaying a disarming self-awareness that has become his norm. "They tended to my insecurities: I was subconsciously seeking attention and approval, but all they did was create a barrier between myself and the world."

"My son," my fellow-facilitator in a conflict resolution session some years ago addressed me as we unwound after the day's work, "when I see the fashions on display around shopping centres, school car parks and office functions - ladies and gents dressed as if they just stepped off a photo set for a glossy mag - I'm pretty much certain that people's inner world is shattered." I was reminded of these words as I wrote about Jonathan. "Striving for outer perfection," this wise colleague of mine - a priest, for what it's worth - told me, "is a tell-tale sign of inner turmoil."

Jonathan's needs for reputation and advancement in his dysfunctional world were a major source of anxiety for him. The more he tried to feed and satisfy them, the more they dug a hole for him. "I felt the outward appearance of intimidation would be a substitute for the lack of heart on my side."

Jonathan's story is a stark example of the influence of anxiety in our lives, and it served as a reminder to me to remain mindful of how it can work for and against us.

Jonathan hadn't been working at the security company for long when a new bouncing company arrived on the scene. To begin with, the two companies shared contracts. Clubs would have "one of our bouncers, one of theirs," Jonathan says. It seemed to Jonathan that this new company was infringing on his boss's territory, so he confronted him. "I said to him, 'Why don't you deal with these guys, not submit to them?'" Jonathan told me. "But he responded with just a look, a silent glare." Jonathan realised he'd touched a nerve.

One night, while Jonathan was on duty at a club, the owner of the new bouncing company put his arm around Jonathan's neck and said, "Lightie, why don't you come and work for us? This field is going to be big, and we're the next best thing."

Feeling important, as though someone had noticed him, Jonathan decided to take up the offer and made the move to the new security company. His old boss, though, took Jonathan's move as a slap in the face. Jonathan shrugged it off. He wanted to be in with the "big boys", and this was his opportunity. "In retrospect," Jonathan tells me in 2020, "I understand how my changing companies was insulting to my ex-boss. But I didn't at the time."

Working at the new bouncing company, Jonathan soon realised he may be in over his head. His colleagues were bouncers he'd previously had some altercations with, but he brushed aside any niggling worries, feeling assured that he was progressing in the life he wanted. He tells me he would tell himself, "One day, I will be like them."

He was causing frustration for his new employers, though. Jonathan admits that he was afraid of his boss and his boss's partners, but he was wilful. He frequently got into fights while on duty, and didn't know where to draw the line. The same was true of his use of drugs and alcohol – he would go overboard. When his boss or colleagues tried to bring him into line, he wouldn't listen.

To Jonathan, he was simply doing what they all did. He thought, "If they can do it, I can do it." He assumed that he could mimic their behaviour, because he was 'one of them'. He wasn't.

It's probably stating the obvious to point out that aggression is a conspicuous thread in the Jonathan Street story. His mother noted Jonathan's aggression had been problematic early on. During high school, Jonathan's experience of bullying led to aggression being met by aggression. That Jonathan actively sought employment and reputation in a realm renowned for its aggressive nature suggests that aggression was a motivating force in Jonathan's life.

Aggression is a normal human response to certain stimuli. All the same, it's a complex phenomenon, with neurobiological, genetic, evolutionary and societal factors interacting to produce behaviours that are hard to correlate directly with causes or accurately predict, despite a long history of cross-disciplinary research.

Although our understanding of aggression is as yet incomplete, there are a few things researchers agree are true about aggression. For one, it's a given that men are more aggressive than women are, even if scientists still differ on whether this is down to nature or nurture. Negative emotions such as fear, anger and frustration can trigger aggressive behaviour in people who are naturally more aggressive. Alcohol and steroid abuse has been positively shown to increase aggression.

It seems to me that Jonathan, starting out with a tendency towards increased aggression, was exposed to – and intentionally sought out – a dangerous combination of factors that only served to fuel the fire of his aggression.

One night, Jonathan's brother got into an altercation with the bouncers at a nightclub they were visiting in a nearby town. He was so badly beaten by the bouncers that he had to walk home. The next day he had no memory of how he got home.

A few days later Jonathan returned to the venue with his brother and a few friends. The same bouncers greeted them in a friendly way and escorted them into the club.

"It was great," Jonathan says.

After they had been there for a few hours, one of the bouncers told Jonathan he wanted to speak to him outside. Jonathan didn't anticipate trouble, "because we were having a good time," he says. But he reached the parking lot and was immediately surrounded by a group of bouncers. A heavy man stepped forward and spoke.

"You think you own this town, hey? You think you're the main oke?"

With that, the guy next to Jonathan struck him on the head with a police cosh, splitting it open. Jonathan was struck again, and again.

Jonathan's brother and friends had been looking for him, and at this point they arrived on the scene and intervened. A fight broke out. Jonathan used the distraction to run, but he was followed by one of the bouncers, who cornered him between two cars.

"Put your hands down!" he yelled, and Jonathan complied. But as the other man got closer, Jonathan caught him with a left hook and fled.

Jonathan was covered in blood and full of rage and adrenaline. Finding his brother and friends, they set off for a club Jonathan regularly worked at to rally his associates to "go back and deal with them." The manager stepped in as Jonathan was talking to his fellow bouncers.

"Look at yourself, Jonathan," he said. "You can't go back. Go home and rest. You're in no state to go anywhere." Jonathan took his advice and went home.

Word of the fight got around, and the bosses of the two rival groups decided to set a place and time to get all those involved together so the matter could be "sorted out." The appointment was set for a parking lot one afternoon; on the agenda, for Jonathan and his friend to face the heavy and police cosh guy respectively to brawl it out.

During our Saturday Sessions, his friends describe Jonathan from those days as a 'typical breeker-type', the kind of tough guy that exudes aggression.

"Jonathan's like a rhinoceros," a close friend of Jonathan's tells me. "He was extremely aggressive, with a thick skin and a horn that was impenetrable."

Other friends used words such as, 'tough', 'street smart' and 'hardened'.

"He simply would not listen to anyone," one of his friends says.

"You couldn't reason with him," said another.

"He was an angry young man," was a frequently repeated statement.

Jonathan himself says, "I was very angry."

I once asked Jonathan which people had influenced him and why. At the top of his list, he answered, was Mike Tyson.

"I was impressed by his power," Jonathan explains, "And the way he could hit."

He was impressed with Tyson's ways out of the ring, too, especially the way the famous boxer reacted to his naysayers when they disrespected him.

"The fear people had for Tyson was something I wanted to cause in others. In conflict situations, I would think, 'If Mike Tyson was here, how would he react?'"

Closer to home, it was the type of guys who had reputations for fighting that Jonathan looked up to.

"It seems strange to me now," he tells me. "Why didn't I choose better role models? The good guys who achieve success through working hard, learning and studying."

The people he worked for were also big influences on Jonathan, his boss at the time of the looming brawl especially.

"I would've done anything for him," he says.

Jonathan wanted to have the same respect and influence his boss had, he tells me. To that end, he'd emulate his boss's bad-boy ways, but this did not sit well with his boss.

"I caused him a lot of aggravation," he admits.

"OK, who's going first?" someone asked, as the meeting convened.

After a moment's silence, Jonathan's friend – "a very good boxer with a lionheart," Jonathan describes him – put up his hand and said, "Me." The audience laughed.

"He's always underestimated by his appearance," Jonathan explains to me as he's telling the story.

The contenders put on their boxing wraps and piled into each other. Jonathan's friend out-boxed, outpowered and dominated his opponent. "They had to pull the lionheart off the other guy... He was giving him a boxing lesson of note!" Jonathan says. "What a sight! I'll never forget it."

It was Jonathan's turn. He took off his shirt, and as he held up his hands for someone to put his wraps on, he looked over to his adversary. The heavy took off his shirt too and began walking towards Jonathan.

"My heart dropped," Jonathan says. "I thought to myself, 'This is a big mistake. What did I get myself into?'"

"This is not a 15 year old, lightie," he heard his boss saying.

"You're in for the hiding of your life!" someone else said. The assembled were heckling Jonathan, but an associate of Jonathan's he admired clapped him on the shoulder.

"Don't listen to all these okes," he told Jonathan. "They're speaking shit. All you need to do is, never give up. OK?"

The heavy was grinning from cheek to massive cheek as the contenders approached each other, and Jonathan tells me he felt like he was going to fight King Kong.

The fight began and Jonathan came in throwing punches, missing every one. The heavy laughed at Jonathan and mocked him. Finally landing a right overhand to his opponent's face, Jonathan gained some confidence, but it was too soon. King Kong came back with a rally of powerful punches which hit their mark over and over again. He grabbed Jonathan and picked him up, swinging him around so that his legs were in the air, and dumped him head-first onto the paving, "Like a ragdoll," Jonathan says.

Jonathan got to his feet, dazed, only to be met with another series of blows that sent him tripping over a step onto a patch of grass. As he pulled himself onto all fours, a kick from the heavy landed hard in his face and his vision swam. He remembered his associate's words, "Never give up," and fought the urge to pass out. He tried to stand up, but kept falling. He remembers thinking, "If I stay down, I'm finished."

The heavy tried to get a choke-hold on Jonathan and Jonathan's boss put his face into his and shouted, "Do you want to stop? Huh? Are you done?"

Looking into his boss's face, Jonathan saw he was getting a kick out of the episode. The realisation that many of those who were supposedly in his corner were hoping he'd lose dawned on him, and he decided not to give them the satisfaction. Jonathan knew that if he surrendered, he'd lose all credibility – with his boss, with his adversaries, with his friends. He was filled with an urge not to repeat his previous cowardice and declined his boss's invitation in the strongest terms, with a few choice expletives.

With renewed determination, Jonathan got to his feet and squared up to his opponent. He threw a risky left-handed punch that would end him if he missed, but it landed and put his opponent on his knees.

"I tried to kick him," Jonathan tells me. "But I was too weak to lift my legs."

The heavy got to his feet again and threw punch after punch. Jonathan managed a blow that broke his opponents nose.

"He started running," Jonathan remembers. "But I was too dizzy. I couldn't chase."

Jonathan's boss gave him a smack, which revitalised him, and he approached the heavy with his hands up, ready to continue.

King Kong's boss intervened, saying the fight was over, Jonathan's opponent was surrendering. Jonathan was filled with euphoria and relief.

"I thought now I would be accepted," he told me. "Belonging, acceptance was paramount to me."

On a different occasion, Jonathan was leaving a club at the end of his shift. He was on the phone, but heard from behind him, "Hey! You poes!" He turned to see who was talking, only to be hit in the face. When he was hit a second time, he turned around and ran. When his assaulter caught up with him, he said, "Lightie, you're dead."

It was his boss. Later, Jonathan would learn, he'd accused Jonathan of bullying his nephew – not true, according to Jonathan. For neither the first time nor the last time in his life, Jonathan felt let down by someone he looked up to, someone he'd hoped would "take him in as one of his own."

"Fuck them," he thought.

V
LOOSE CANNON

Jonathan and I had been working together on the book for some "I would see all these heavy guys with guns and I desperately wanted one."

While he was still under 21 years of age, Jonathan needed his parents' permission to apply for a license.

"I asked my father if he would sign for me to get a gun, but he refused. So many times."

In June 2002, Jonathan turned 21 and immediately applied for a license for a .45 Colt.

"I couldn't wait until I finally got it. It was all I wanted at the time."

"Jonathan loved the bling and the ladies," a friend tells me during a Saturday Session.

Jonathan's friends and associates I met remembered the negative qualities he displayed at the time, and weren't shy to talk about them either. Partying, fighting and womanising filled his time when he wasn't bouncing, they say, describing him as being unable to settle down.

"He was always looking for the next thing," says one.

"The steroids and drugs affected him badly," says another.

"He had a short temper."

"He did as he liked."

"I wanted to be known for my ability to fight," Jonathan himself remembers.

"I was full of complexities and insecurities," he tells me in an email in 2020. "And my steroid use wasn't helping." He describes himself then as "living in a bubble. I thought my life was the way the world was."

The summer break and Christmas rolled around, and most of the bouncing fraternity left Johannesburg for holiday spots around the country. Jonathan had no money to go away. Off duty one night, he and some friends were partying at one of their houses when Jonathan got a call: one of their mates was in trouble and needed help. Jonathan and some friends hopped into a car and headed for the location: a restaurant in the north of Johannesburg.

On arriving, Jonathan saw his friend who needed help outside the restaurant with a man he didn't recognise. He got out of the car and approached, saying, "Hey, what's the problem here?"

"Lightie, watch your fucking mouth!" the other guy said.

"Excuse me?" Jonathan replied, getting into the other guy's face. Did Jonathan strike the first blow, or the stranger? Regardless, a fight started and all the guys piled in.

The stranger fled and Jonathan and his mates set off in chase. By the time Jonathan reached him, the others had continued the brawl. Jonathan got involved, and before long, the man was severely injured. Realising he was unconscious, Jonathan and company fled the scene.

Jonathan and his friends panicked. They considered reporting the incident to the police, but feared the repercussions.

"I thought I'd end up in prison," he says.

They decided to lay low and went into hiding, but the time was fraught and they had many arguments.

A day or two later, Jonathan saw the incident reported on the front page of The Star. He and his friend, the article said, were wanted in connection with murder.

"I couldn't believe this was happening," Jonathan says. "It was like the movies: seeing yourself on the front page. I was shocked... I mean, yes, I wanted to have a reputation... But this was another level."

Jonathan skipped the country with his fellow suspect. Panic and anxiety followed him, and he couldn't settle. He travelled around, restless and fearful, sleeping little and binging on alcohol and drugs.

There came a time when he and his friend decided to part ways. Jonathan stayed in hiding overseas while his friend returned to South Africa and turned himself in.

Alone and far away, Jonathan had little knowledge about what was happening back home. Talking to his previous boss one day, he learnt that he was the only one of the accused that was still on the run. His fellow offenders had been acquitted of the charges. "You need to turn yourself in," Jonathan's boss advised.

Jonathan reasoned that he can't run forever and he made arrangements to come home and face the music. He applied for bail at the Randburg Magistrate's court early in 2004 and it was set at R20 000.

"Street was back walking the streets," he says wryly. "How crazy was that?"

As I got to know Jonathan Street during the winter of 2020, I became accustomed to his self-deprecating sense of humour.

Not surprisingly, Jonathan's friends and family report that he was not a happy chappie back in those turbulent times. He seldom smiled, they said, and he was angry a lot. Consequently, he was increasingly aggressive and hostile. Jonathan himself remembers an incident in 2004 when he laughed at something, and a close friend said, "That's the first time I've seen you laugh." Many years later, in 2010, a friend asked Jonathan to smile for a photograph.

"That's the first time I remember smiling for a photograph."

Six years between those comments. That's over 2 000 days. Over 52 000 hours.

I couldn't imagine an hour without a smile, a giggle or a laugh. It's one way we can manage our stresses and anxieties, and I almost always feel better after the release. We live in a time in which there is so much to laugh about, however sardonically. If you don't find the antics of politicians, celebrities, your boss, your friends or your family funny, try laughing at yourself. I told Jonathan I thought he could teach many people who take themselves far too seriously to poke fun at themselves. It made him chuckle.

Despite the high anxiety of the time, Jonathan thought it was fantastic to be out on bail. His pride grew and he felt in charge again. Perhaps even invincible.

Bumping into an old connection a few days later, Jonathan learnt that his gun license had been approved. He wasted no time and set off to collect his license and weapon: a pitch black Colt .45.

"I was out on bail, charged with murder, and now I was in possession of a licensed firearm."

Out of work and restless, Jonathan initially stayed at a friend's place, but that didn't last long. Feeling as though he was getting in the way, he moved from place to place, returning to his father's house for a while, and eventually taking up residence with acquaintances in Pretoria who were drug dealers and sworn enemies of his erstwhile colleagues.

He managed to land some work as a bouncer, but continued to party hard.

"When you have friends who manufacture and sell narcotics," he observes, "life seems to take you to different places."

He continued to drink excessively and find himself embroiled in fights, despite the conditions of his bail. His behaviour deteriorated, and after making passes at friends' girlfriends and pissing guys off by shooting his mouth off, he became more and more isolated.

Jonathan met up with one of his brother's close friends, who helped him secure some work in debt collecting.

"I owe him," Jonathan says. "He's a strong guy with a magnificent heart, my best friend today." This friend stepped in to help Jonathan and his brother on multiple occasions. "He will always be dear to me. He loves me like no other."

Things in his circle had changed while Jonathan had been overseas, and he observed that his associates had forged new alliances and embarked on new ventures, an observation that served to make him feel excluded.

Jonathan describes himself during those times as a "lone ranger", one of his friends described him as a "loose cannon".

Issues that had cropped up from Jonathan's time on the run had not been resolved, and he began frustrating his ex-bosses, making trouble. Discord and violence seemed to follow Jonathan wherever he went, and he was racking up more enemies in the process. Soon, he heard a rumour that he was "being looked for", and his fear and paranoia would only serve to send him running to the next gram.

As his world closed in on him, Jonathan had no interest in the consequences of his actions, and no time horizon that stretched further than the end of the day. He withdrew, avoiding others, and fuelling his paranoia and ego by learning to fight.

"Jonathan was out of control," is what I heard from many of his friends about the time, one adding, "It got worse as his court case drew closer."

"He was always looking for something," she said. "Wanting the next thing. He was always involved in something, into this and that."

"I was on my way to self-destruction," Jonathan says.

Jonathan took some comfort from the fact that he was "packing a Colt .45." His weapon brought him a new sense of security.

VI
AWAITING TRIAL

"Choices," Jonathan reflects in 2020, "have consequences. We complicate life with our bad choices and crisis management."

The consequences of our choices are sometimes hard to swallow, he admits.

"I did stupid things which I've paid for in so many ways."

Moving out of Johannesburg to stay with his mother and her boyfriend in another province seemed a practical way to get away from the crowd, from Johannesburg, and from the paranoia.

"I couldn't do it anymore," Jonathan says. "Enough was enough."

Jonathan left, hoping it would improve things, and spent three months living with his mother and helping her boyfriend do renovations. He thought his fortunes had changed for the better. Visiting Johannesburg for a weekend, Jonathan and his brother went to a friend's house for a party.

"It was fun," he says. The people there were friendly and warm towards him.

After some drinks, the party relocated to a bar, but it seemed Jonathan's history would follow him. As had so often happened in the past, Jonathan got into a fight. When the music was stopped and the lights were switched on, he realised he needed to leave. As he exited the bar, he drew his firearm and fired two shots into the ground.

He was due in court a week later on a Monday morning, and he thought it would be easiest to return to Johannesburg the next weekend to be close. He slept at his dad's place on Friday night, and on Saturday morning, his dad handed over his credit card and said he should take his brother out for breakfast. This was something that had never happened before. Jonathan took his dad's credit card.

"Check the last three numbers," he said. "They're 666."

"Ag, it's nothing, man. Just a number," his dad said. "Forget about it."

Jonathan and his brother went to Eastgate. Jonathan decided to order a drink with breakfast.

"Please don't get drunk," Jonathan remembers his brother asking.

As they waited for their food to arrive, Jonathan saw a friend he hadn't seen for some time. They greeted each other, chatted for a bit, and exchanged numbers. Jonathan agreed to call him that evening to meet up.

The brothers spent the rest of the day driving around, drinking, bored. On impulse, Jonathan decided to stop at a gun shop to buy some rounds. He'd been carrying Black Talon ammunition, and he'd begun to think it may be risky.

At some point during the course of the day, Jonathan's brother told him that a friend of Jonathan's ex-boss had made sexual passes at him. Jonathan called his ex-boss up immediately, telling him he was looking for his friend, and that he would "put a bullet in-between his eyes."

"Lightie, are you high again?" was all his ex-boss had to say.

It was drawing towards evening when Jonathan called his buddy and suggested they meet at a nearby casino. After a few triples and shooters, his mate suggested they go to a bar, and the three of them ventured out to the same bar Jonathan had visited the week before. The bouncers there refused to allow Jonathan to enter because of the previous incident, so the trio changed their plans, heading off for a strip club in a nearby town.

The bar at the strip club was filled with bikers and girls. After a drink at the bar, Jonathan left his mate and brother to retire to one of the private rooms upstairs with a girl he'd picked up. He returned to the bar sometime later, and when he didn't find his companions, continued drinking.

It was the early hours of Sunday morning, and Jonathan was supposed to be attending a christening in just a few hours. His looming court date on Monday was also weighing on Jonathan's mind, so he decided to pay his bill and leave to find his brother and friend. His father's credit card was declined.

Irritated, Jonathan left. He waited for his brother and friend on the pavement outside, but when they didn't appear, he went back inside to find them.

On entering the club, Jonathan saw his brother on his hands and knees on the floor, being kicked in the face by a biker. Jonathan leapt to his brother's defence and smacked the biker. The biker returned with a right hook, and got Jonathan into a headlock against the bar. While the two were battling, Jonathan noticed his buddy unconscious under a nearby table. He railed against the biker's hold on him as more punches rained down on him. He couldn't get loose and he reached for his weapon. With the other man's arm still around his neck, Jonathan fired a warning shot into the ceiling.

The biker reacted by keeping a hold on Jonathan, squeezing tighter and tighter around his neck. Jonathan fired another shot, then managed to break free of the headlock. As he regained his balance, he fired a third shot in the direction of the biker and his crewmates.

The bullet hit a young man, who fell to the ground.

The club was in chaos. Jonathan's brother and friends regained consciousness, and they all fled along with the staff and patrons.

Jonathan and his companions drove directly to the house of a friend of his, and Jonathan handed over his firearm, asking his friend to take it to Jonathan's father. From there, Jonathan and his brother went to attend the christening.

Jonathan remembers the experience of sitting in the church that morning, surrounded by happy families taking part in an event filled with joy and love, and thinking to himself that this was the last day he would ever see the outside world.

Following the christening, Jonathan returned to drinking, later calling some friends to join him. He spent the rest of the day and the whole night drunk and high, and as the sun rose on Monday morning, he went to the Randburg Magistrates Court to stand trial for the murder case he was on bail for.

Jonathan met his lawyer, who accompanied him into the building. On seeing a number of uniformed police officers inside, he told his lawyer that they were there to arrest him. His lawyer told Jonathan that he was being paranoid.

VII
GUILTY

After Jonathan's return to South Africa from life on the run, he became very familiar with the inside of the courtroom. But, "After every court appearance," he tells me in 2020, "it would just be some more time bought... Until the next time." In between, he'd continue with his thuggish ways, fighting, drinking, getting high, paying no attention to the terms of his bail.

One moment in court in particular stands out in Jonathan's memory with absolute clarity, though. He was on trial for murder, and while court was adjourned for a tea break, he was chatting with a friend. Jonathan doesn't remember what they were talking about, but he remembers he was laughing.

Out of the corner of his eye, Jonathan saw the mother of the man he was accused of murdering.

Turning to look at her, Jonathan saw she was watching him.

"It was like she was just a body," he says. "She was empty, like a zombie."

Perhaps for the first time, Jonathan considered what he'd done from a different perspective. The weight of his responsibility for this woman's sadness landed on him with a jolt. He realised how inappropriate his laughter was; had an inkling of what this mother's pain must be.

"I realised it was me who'd destroyed this woman."

Part 2:

INCARCERATION

VIII
DOING TIME

Jonathan was sentenced to 15 years' imprisonment and taken down to the holding cells before being transported to the Johannesburg prison nicknamed Sun City.

In the police van en route to Sun City, Jonathan began to prepare himself for the conflict and turmoil that he was certain was imminent. He was scared, angry and frustrated.

"I had no hope," he tells me.

He told himself over and over that he wouldn't allow himself to be harmed while in jail.

On arrival, Jonathan's clothes were taken from him and he was given the orange alternatives.

"I'd never seen anything like it," he says of his first impression of prison. "It was a full, tense place. So many people, so much movement." The people, he says, had "empty faces".

He was taken to the kitchen and given food, but he couldn't face eating. He hadn't slept for two nights and his system was still full of drugs. Psychologically, Jonathan had never before experienced being on edge like he was at that moment.

One afternoon in 2020, I asked Jonathan what his greatest fears were at the time, and his response had been a single word: "Prison."

My parents loved prison movies, and we spent many a dreary Sunday throughout the 70s and 80s watching them through our cranky VCR. I'll never forget the old man chopping his fingers off in *Escape from Alcatraz*, and *Shawshank Redemption* remains one of my favourite films of all time. Morgan Freeman's character calling chess a "total fucking mystery" still has me barrelling over, even after over a hundred views.

Hollywood could not have prepared me for my own experience of incarceration, though.

After one whiskey too many at a newly opened establishment near my home a few years ago, I made the noble decision to walk the roughly one-kilometre home rather than risk driving inebriated. Leather briefcase in hand, my jacket slung over my arm, I was trekking up the hill when I was stopped by a pair of law enforcement officers.

"Hey," one said gruffly to me. "Have you been drinking?"

"I have," I replied with some pride, "and that's why I'm walking home and not driving."

Instead of the enthusiastic encouragement I'd expected from the officer, he informed me that "Walking while over the limit is still illegal."

Before I'd recovered from my surprise at this information, I found myself in the back of the police van. Perhaps to aid me in sobering up, perhaps to fill me with fear, the officers drove around for some time before heading for the charge office. On assisting me out of the back of the van, the officer described a means for me to avoid what was coming, and when I politely declined, I was unceremoniously flung into a four-by-four cell to reflect on my transgressions.

I spent about six unanswered hours in that cell, just a crusty grey blanket and bright overhead light for company, and around 3 am I was pulled out to be released.

While the paperwork was being seen to, I struck up a conversation with a fellow inmate. I asked him why he'd been locked up, and he replied that he'd been caught shoplifting a few hundred grams of mozzarella from the local supermarket. "Mozzarella?!" I remember being surprised. "Why mozzarella?"

His reply was quick. "Well," he said matter-of-factly. "Cheddar is full of fat and other processed stuff. I prefer the Italian variety. It's healthier."

Since my vehicle remained in the parking lot of the place of my impropriety, I was given a ride home by a charming officer who allowed me to switch on the blue lights as we sped up the hill. She drew the line at my request to turn on the siren, though. I see her from time to time at the filling station down the road from me, and we always giggle about the incident.

I make light of my experience, but those six long hours were enough to convince me that prison is a terrifying place. I completely understood Jonathan's fear of being locked up.

"Jonathan!"

Jonathan turned to see who was calling him and saw a white guy with a cap and gold earrings.

"Just relax, OK? I'll check you now."

A little while later, the guy returned, introducing himself and asking Jonathan how he was doing, reminding him to relax.

"Everything's going to be fine," he said. "Come."

Jonathan followed his new friend to a cell where a bed had been prepared for him. He was introduced to a couple of fellow inmates who helped him get settled. The guys gave him a rundown of how prison worked and what to expect, and organised everything he needed.

An inmate from the cell next to Jonathan's approached him, asking many questions about life on the outside. It turned out he had also been a bouncer, and he and Jonathan knew a lot of people in common. He invited Jonathan to train with him in the prison gym.

Jonathan was relieved by this introduction to prison and felt the reality was much better than what he had anticipated. His basic needs were met, and he had a friend to spend time with. His new-found mate who'd been expecting him did not stay in the communal cell section of the prison as Jonathan did, but he arrived every morning to fetch Jonathan and take him to the single cell section where he stayed. There they would prepare food and eat together, and the two got to know each other well.

"I didn't feel I had to prove myself," Jonathan says of the friendship.

Despite these small comforts, adjusting to incarceration was a stressful time for Jonathan. It wasn't even a case of gritting teeth and getting through it, Jonathan says. He didn't believe he'd be getting out any time soon, because of the pending case. To manage the anxiety, Jonathan kept himself occupied by training in the gym and boxing to keep fit.

"I wasn't really making progress," Jonathan says of this time. "I was just passing each day as it came." He'd wake up each morning at five and prepare for the day, showering and dressing with care. He'd be at the gym as soon as they opened every morning; every other afternoon, he'd box.

Inmates would spend up to sixteen hours a day behind bars if all went well, more if it didn't. Cells were open during the daytime hours between 7 am and 2 pm, and inmates would keep each other company, chatting and joking to pass the time and make the days more tolerable.

"I met so many people there," Jonathan says. "Characters, strange people, people like I didn't know existed... most of the guys I met there were gangsters." He describes the inmates as mostly "cold in the heart." He continues, "There are good people inside. But they are rare."

Once, Jonathan met an inmate with half his face missing, his front teeth implants. When he asked what had happened, the guy laughed and said he'd been shot in the face.

"Like it was a joke," Jonathan says.

The gangsters in prison, Jonathan tells me, were "fast with their mouths... and with their actions." They hung around in groups and were friendly, but Jonathan soon figured out they would engage with ulterior motives.

"In prison," he says. "You learn how to use your mind, not your fists." On another occasion, he says, "You start to read people accurately."

Jonathan had a roommate who was a gangster and well respected, giving him a small advantage in this new and threatening environment.

"I didn't feel as if I was alone against the others."

The conflict Jonathan had anticipated in prison was not as he thought it would be. Just as on the outside, there are rules on the inside, and behaving badly or getting into fights would lead to punishment doled out by the officials. Conflict that may have led to a physical fight while he was free had to be managed differently if Jonathan didn't want to suffer the consequences.

"People with short tempers," he says, "will be tested every day." During one of our Saturday Sessions, he says, "It's a good way to overcome your weaknesses. You'll be faced with them all the time."

The highlight of life in prison was the hour-long weekly visits, if you were fortunate to have a guest. Many inmates, Jonathan says, had none. Jonathan found the lack of love and affection in prison one of his greatest difficulties. A friend who visited him frequently through his years inside said to me more than once, "Jonathan is a gentle being with a massive heart."

Prisoners initially receive guests through glass windows for about six months before becoming eligible to receive contact visits. Jonathan's visitors in those early days of his imprisonment often cried, he says.

"But it was great to see your own people, the people who love you."

Jonathan often had visits from a lady he'd met a few weeks before he went to prison. She was relaxed, funny and loyal, and her visits helped Jonathan considerably. She supported him financially for a number of years, and Jonathan says she was instrumental in helping him survive.

"I will be eternally grateful to her," he says.

"There's an invisible, unwritten code that prevails in prison," Jonathan tells me. 'Inside' has its own culture, and as Jonathan learnt how to make his way within it, he became quite comfortable. "You share your things," he tells me, adding that he and his mates shared everything. "If you help somebody with something, they'll do the same back," he adds.

I've observed the power of implicit culture in corporates and institutions. The 'real' rules are almost always unwritten. Policies, procedures, processes and values can be sloganised all over the place, but it's the unwritten that drives behaviour.

Jonathan's friend with the earrings didn't like Jonathan hanging around with his ex-bouncer neighbour. He recommended Jonathan apply to be moved to the single cells section, where the lifestyle was much better. Jonathan's application was successful, but after just three short months, he got into a conflict with another inmate and had to move back to the communal cells.

IX
A TOUCH OF GRACE

Jonathan's friend who'd been expecting him on that first day in prison was good to him, loyal. He had more experience in prison than Jonathan had, and was accustomed to how things worked. He wasn't afraid of anyone. Jonathan noticed, however, that he'd often find him alone.

"I only understood why years later," he says. I encourage him to elaborate. "You get tired of all the disappointments, in prison," he explains. "Guys pretend to be friends with you, they seem to care. But you open up to them and regret it. Over and over again. You learn to be more reserved. You start to anticipate other people's ulterior motives."

His heart was broken many times in prison, Jonathan says, each time leaving him more disappointed and frustrated. He knew his friend and others he knew were troubled by the same experiences, his friend's hopelessness exacerbated by the thought that his time of release would never come.

"Hey, Jonathan. You could organise to get some ecstasy in here for us, couldn't you?"

Jonathan was in the cell he shared with about two dozen others. He knew he could probably do what his cellmate had asked, so he got off his bed to go down the length of the cell to a group of inmates seated near the toilet to talk about the possibility of buying the drug.

"My mind was directing me to these guys, on the left," he tells me. But as he passed the cell's Bible study section on the right, where a few Christian brothers were gathered, "I felt something pull me in that direction."

On impulse, Jonathan joined the assembled inmates on the right-hand side. They welcomed him, "as if they knew I was on my way to them," he says. "I sat down with brothers I didn't even know and they laid hands on me and we prayed."

Jonathan describes this event as the moment he received his faith. As the inmates prayed over him, "I heard His voice, and I felt a great peace in my spirit.

"I was born again," Jonathan says. "I accepted Jesus Christ as my Lord and Saviour." He quotes John 15:16, "You did not choose me, but I chose you…"

X
TROUBLED WATERS

"I'd heard God speak to me many times in my life," Jonathan tells me one day. "But I didn't listen. I was ignorant and disobedient."

Following Jonathan's spiritual rebirth, he began to attend church and regularly gathered with the Christian group.

"I started reading the "Word", and got to know Jesus more," he tells me. "Most of us have been to church on a Sunday and listened to what the pastor says with enjoyment, because it's uplifting, and then we leave feeling redeemed."

But Jonathan wanted a deeper understanding of the Bible.

"I wanted to know the "Word" for myself and to know how to differentiate between the truth and error."

In March 2008, just over a year after being incarcerated, Jonathan was sentenced to a further 24 years imprisonment for the shooting at the strip club.

This was shortly followed by another pivotal event in Jonathan's life: his baptism.

The Sun City prison church organised an event for all the inmates who wanted to be baptised. Needing a venue that would allow members to be fully submerged under water, the hospital was chosen for the ceremony, where Jonathan and his fellow believers could be baptised in the baths.

"It was a lovely event," Jonathan says. "After I came out of the water, I could see the Spirit hovering in that place."

Then, one ordinary day in 2008, Jonathan's name appeared on a list of transfers: he was to be moved from Sun City to Zonderwater Correctional Services, a prison about an hour and a half drive from Johannesburg.

By this time, Jonathan and his mate had become very close. It was difficult for Jonathan to think of leaving, but he felt a new environment would be good for him. His friend, however, was deeply unhappy about Jonathan's pending transferral, even approaching the prison officials to try to persuade them to allow Jonathan to stay.

The journey to Zonderwater seemed to take forever. Jonathan was not used to the sensation of being in a vehicle. It was hot and the road was bumpy, the smell of petrol was nauseating. After a few hours of discomfort, they arrived.

The new prison was clean and fresh, neater than the previous one. Jonathan was admitted and shown to his cell, and in no time he began to be approached by inquisitive inmates, each wanting to know what his crime was, his name, and how many years he was sentenced to – in that order.

The cells in this institution opened right onto an open grass field, and inmates could play a number of different sports. As Jonathan settled into his new home, he enjoyed spending time in the sun and playing sports.

He kept mostly to himself and did his best to get along with everyone. It worked, for the most part, but he did find fellow prisoners would sometimes try to intimidate him.

"In prison," he tells me, "you're judged mainly on appearance. If you're handsome, if you have a pretty face, you're assumed to be a pushover. But you never know the road an inmate has walked."

Jonathan found it challenging to manage these interactions, knowing that attempts at intimidation were the precursor to attempts to take advantage.

"Prison is different from outside," he says. "If someone provokes you, you can't just retaliate or leave. You have to live with the same people, in the same cell, day in and day out."

There's conflict in prison on a daily basis, Jonathan explains. It's not always serious, but it results in continuous tension.

In time, Jonathan managed to make friends in Zonderwater. One fellow inmate – "another person with a good heart," says Jonathan – frequently invited him to join him playing sport on the field. As he got to know his new friend, Jonathan discovered he was a talented individual, as skilled at drawing as he was at soccer.

He began to coach Jonathan in boxing and taught him a great deal. In one boxing lesson, he connected with Jonathan's nose and broke it. As the blood streamed from Jonathan's nose, his friend's anxiety increased. "Does my nose look straighter?" Jonathan asked him. The boxer looked at him with confusion for a moment, and then he said,

"Yes, it actually does."

"Well, then I should thank you."

Jonathan hadn't been at Zonderwater long when his new friend was transferred to a medium security facility. It was a painful time for Jonathan.

Another inmate tried to bully and intimidate Jonathan over the use of a public phone. The incident escalated and he and Jonathan were both sent to isolation cells.

37

"It was extremely challenging," Jonathan says. "You lose track of time, locked up on your own most of the day. The only company I had was a bright light. I'd fall asleep and wake up thinking it was the next day, but it would be later the same day."

Prison requires a mentality of survival and self-preservation, Jonathan tells me. He remembers one character from the Zonderwater days, a highly intelligent and strategic individual that Jonathan never saw eye to eye with, though he tried.

"He was doing a long sentence," Jonathan explains. "And he was focused on life inside."

This inmate liked to dominate and intimidate people, using his smart mouth and menacing looks to maintain an image and be feared. He was in many fights, "as if he had something to prove."

Interestingly, "The world outside prison," Jonathan tells me, "is much more dangerous in terms of the risk of physical fights. The people who intimidated me on the outside were more violent than those on the inside."

In time, two new inmates who had been involved in a high-profile case arrived at Zonderwater. Jonathan observed that they looked uncomfortable with the transition from the outside world and befriended them. He soon learned that one was a rugby player, the other a bodybuilder, and the three began playing sports together. "They were physically and mentally strong," Jonathan remembers. "They came from good families and they were Christians." Jonathan admired his two new friends, despite the fact that they were younger than him. Sharing a cell with them was the highlight of his prison sentence.

Jonathan began teaching the pair to box, and soon enough, they were returning the favour by teaching him too. "The training and conversations with them helped me escape my situation."

When they, too, were transferred to a medium security facility, Jonathan had a difficult time. "I became so close to them," he says, "I cried so much when they left. I was happy for them, but it felt like a part of me left with them."

XI
PRAYER FOR REDEMPTION

"I cried," Jonathan tells me in 2020. "I often cried, thinking about what I'd done in the past and all the people I'd hurt along the way."

The lack of affection in prison was one of the hardest aspects of Jonathan's incarceration. Knowing he had a visit coming on the weekend, knowing it would make him feel loved and wanted, was how he managed to push through the week.

"There were some inmates," he tells me, "who never received a visit. I couldn't imagine the pain and rejection they must have felt."

Jonathan had found solace in his God and companionship among fellow Christian inmates, but he longed for a wife.

"I prayed to God," he tells me. "I told Him, 'I'm ready.' I said to him that I wasn't concerned about my current situation, about the barriers, the walls and the years I still had left before my release."

Jonathan's increasing commitment to his own growth naturally led to him beginning to preach to his fellow inmates.

"Jesus has called sinners to repentance," he explains, adding, "There is no greater honour than leading someone to Christ."

Repentance is an important theme of the Abrahamic religions (Christianity, Judaism and Islam, among others), and analogous practices are found in other world religions. From a psychological perspective, the features of repentance are essential to change and personal growth: As individuals, we cannot meet our full potential without the acknowledgement of our failures, acceptance of responsibility for the consequences of our actions, and a sincere commitment to changing our behaviour.

In 2012, a professor visiting from the United States facilitated a course at Zonderwater called "Get out and stay out".

"It was life-changing," Jonathan says.

The professor had been incarcerated in America for twenty years, leaving prison with the goal of transforming lives. The programme focussed on helping inmates prepare for life after prison, and it gave Jonathan the attitudinal and behavioural skills needed to propel him in the right direction.

The "Get out and stay out" programme taught Jonathan about criminogenic needs, the characteristics and conditions that are dynamic risk factors influencing an individual's likelihood to exhibit criminal behaviour, or commit another crime following release from prison. Criminogenic needs are: antisocial personality, antisocial attitudes and values, antisocial associates, family dysfunctionality, poor self-control / problem-solving skills, substance abuse, and lack of employment / employment skills.

Jonathan realised that he ticked all the criminogenic needs boxes.

It was becoming apparent to Jonathan that he would need to address his criminogenic needs if he was to leave prison with any potential for a new life.

XII
MOVING ON

In 2014, Jonathan was transferred to Pretoria Central Prison.

Waiting in the visiting area with a nervous fellow inmate from Zonderwater while their admission was being processed, Jonathan looked up and saw a flock of pigeons gathered on a metal bar. Right in the middle of the pigeons was a white dove.

"It was beautiful," he says.

He nudged his companion and pointed.

"Look," he said. "It's a sign. Everything's going to be fine."

The two were taken to the same section of the facility, where an inmate welcomed them by saying, "This place is hell. You're going to sleep on the floor together like sardines."

Jonathan's companion's anxiety increased, but Jonathan comforted him, saying, "Don't worry. Wherever we go, Jesus is with us."

Among all the new faces at Pretoria Central, Jonathan recognised some inmates from Sun City and Zonderwater. One in particular he was pleased to be reunited with, "A clever guy," Jonathan says. "One of the cleverest people I've ever met."

To Jonathan's delight, the new prison had an excellent gym, and he and his clever friend began training together.

Not long after Jonathan's arrival at Pretoria Central, two brothers he'd known on the outside were admitted. One became Jonathan's cellmate, and it was good for Jonathan to have his company. "Both brothers were really big and strong, and Jonathan's cellmate would wrestle with him, throwing him around "like it was nothing," Jonathan says.

Things were feeling good for Jonathan. One day, while he was lying on his bed, awake, he vividly heard a voice saying, "If your ways please me, then I will be with you." Sometime later, he received a vision: A blonde woman standing with two blonde children. There was wood in the background. Their faces were not clear, but Jonathan sensed that this was his future wife.

On one occasion, a friend of Jonathan's from the outside came to visit with a woman friend of his. It was a pleasant visit, Jonathan remembers, full of laughter. When he returned to his section, Jonathan phoned his friend to thank him for the visit, asking for his woman friend's number so that he could thank her too.

Jonathan phoned the woman, and during the course of the call, she told him that a friend of hers had known Jonathan some years ago, and wanted to reconnect. Jonathan was happy to oblige, and he'd occasionally phone this contact from before to chat.

Part 3:

RESPITE

XIII
CHRISSIE

"Chrissie, pack yourself a bag, girlfriend. I'm fetching you for a kuier."

It was late 2014, and Chrissie was keen. She put down the phone and followed her friend's orders, flinging her overnight bag into the trunk twenty minutes later and hopping into the passenger seat.

As they were about to pull out of the driveway, Chrissie's friend's phone rang. She answered cheerfully and began chatting away. Chrissie noticed something different about her friend as she spoke: she seemed so happy. She ignored Chrissie's meaningful looks and mouthed questions about who she was talking to, pushing Chrissie's hand away when she tried to grab the phone to see who was on the other side.

"Listen, can we talk later?" Chrissie's friend said into the phone. "I can't speak right now."

She said goodbye, put down the phone and drove out the driveway.

"Who was that?" Chrissie demanded playfully as they hit the road. "What's going on?" Her friend gave Chrissie a look.

After a moment's silence, she said, "Jonathan Street."

"Jonathan Street?!" Chrissie was alarmed. "Are you mad?"

Chrissie knew Jonathan's brother, and she'd often see him through mutual friends. She'd been living overseas when Jonathan was incarcerated, but she'd since heard stories about how he'd changed, how he was pastoring in prison and helping other inmates do good.

"But I still thought it was a joke," she tells me in 2020. "The way everyone was speaking so highly of someone who'd destroyed people's lives."

Chrissie could see she'd made her friend angry.

"So what?" her friend said, keeping her eyes on the road.

"So what?! The guy's a murderer. Why are you even giving him the time of day?"

"Chrissie, you're such a hypocrite," Chrissie's friend said. "You're so judgemental."

Chrissie gasped. "Rubbish," she said. "Talking to him is asking for trouble."

"You know," Chrissie's friend said. "You're always talking about forgiveness. You call yourself a Christian. But when I tell you I'm talking to an inmate in prison, your sanctimonious attitude clicks in and that all goes out the window. That's why I didn't want to tell you who I was talking to."

What Chrissie's friend said had hurt and it stayed with her. During the course of the visit, Chrissie made some observations: her friend really did seem different. Chrissie couldn't help noticing a bible next to her friend's bed. Maybe she had a point?

Just a few months earlier, Chrissie's grandmother had died.

"That was the start of my spiritual journey," she tells me.

She and her twin sister had been at their grandmother's side when she passed.

"It was so sad," she says. "But we both saw a bright white light as she died, and we felt at peace.

"My granny always tried to teach me forgiveness," Chrissie continues. "She used to say there's no point holding grudges with people who have hurt you, that holding onto pain for too long is pointless. At the time, I didn't understand why it was so important to her."

A short time later, Chrissie was driving home after working late in the office one evening, when she heard a professor talking on the radio.

"It was surprising," she says, "because the car radio was always tuned to 5fm. But for some reason, that night, it was on YFM."

The professor was telling a story about how his wife had been gang raped in front of him, and how the incident had destroyed both their lives.

"He said that one day, while he and his wife were waiting in a queue at a supermarket, she turned to him and said that she needed to forgive those people for what they did. And they did. There and then, the professor and his wife forgave them.

"Gee whizz," Chrissie says. "I can honestly say the tears were rolling down my face."

Chrissie was so moved by the story she was hearing, she had to stop the car on the side of the road.

"I was crying uncontrollably, thinking about how a human being can treat another so badly, how it's possible to ruin other people's lives. But then the professor said that after fifteen years, a massive dark cloud was lifted from their shoulders and their lives changed again for the better as they went on the forgiveness journey.

"It made me think of my granny, and everything she used to say suddenly made sense."

As if her life was following a script, these events were followed by Chrissie being contacted by someone she'd been at school with.

"He'd been the school bully," Chrissie explains. "And he'd given me such a hard time all through my school career."

The bully was making contact to ask Chrissie for her forgiveness.

"Of course I forgave him. But I probably wouldn't have if it wasn't for my gran and that professor on the radio."

Chrissie's friend was chatting to Jonathan again later that same day in November when she said, "Hey, Jonathan, speak to my friend Chrissie," and put the phone to Chrissie's ear.

"I got such a fright," Chrissie admits. "My heart was beating fast and my mouth was dry. My legs were like jelly. I thought, *How did I end up on the phone with someone who's in prison for shooting somebody? What am I supposed to say? What will people think of me?*"

Chrissie started the conversation by asking, "Why are you in prison?"

Her question was followed by a long silence.

"I thought, *Why did I say that?*" Chrissie remembers.

Jonathan eventually replied.

"I'm not going to lie," he said. "I'll never change the story to make it look pretty. The truth is not pleasant."

As Jonathan shared his story with Chrissie on the phone she began to cry.

"He sounded remorseful," she says.

He went on to tell her about the programmes he'd been involved with while in prison, and how he'd received his faith. And then he described to her how he "went through his forgiveness journey." Chrissie was taken aback by his choice of words.

XIV
UP THE N3 IN A NORTHERLY DIRECTION

"She asked so many questions," Jonathan says of Chrissie when they first met by phone. "She wanted to know about everything, about prison, about my life before prison."

He told her she could ask any question she wanted, and he was comfortable answering them all. At the end of their chat, Jonathan asked Chrissie if he could call her from time to time. She agreed and gave him her number.

Prior to speaking to Jonathan, Chrissie hadn't known much about him.

"People didn't speak about Jonathan too much," she says. "But whenever people I knew had been to visit him, they always returned in good spirits.

"I later kicked myself for never asking questions or entertaining the topic," she says. "But I believe all good things happen in the right time. Looking back now, I had to go through everything I went through to be at that exact moment."

Jonathan called Chrissie every day he could and their relationship blossomed by phone. Chrissie had told Jonathan that she was Greek, so he assumed she had dark hair. But one day she mentioned she was blonde, and Jonathan was reminded of his vision of the woman with two children. A few days later, Jonathan had another vision: He and Chrissie were entering a house, and immediately inside the door were two hooks to hang jackets on. When Jonathan shared his vision with Chrissie, she told him her house had just those two hooks inside the door, situated exactly as Jonathan had described.

Chrissie works in real estate, and at the time she was helping a couple find a rental. One day, the couple told Chrissie that they'd had a vision of her: She was in a house with her children. Jonathan had by now told Chrissie of his earlier vision of the blonde woman and her two children, and she thought of that as she explained to the couple that she had no children. When she asked the couple for more information about their vision, they told her there were two children, they were girls, and they were both blonde.

49

At this time, Jonathan decided it was time to finish school. He knew in his heart that he needed to fill his mind and his soul with new life and new things. People had suggested before that he should get his matric, study further, but he'd refused.

"I didn't see the importance of education," he says.

But the friends he'd made during his time in prison had been more educated than he was, and he began to realise that he needed to think about his employability when he would finally be released. He'd taken part in various educational programmes throughout his incarceration, and he had experienced how these had helped him grow, "intellectually, spiritually, emotionally and mentally," he says. But the idea was daunting.

After they had been chatting by phone for a few weeks, Jonathan and Chrissie thought it was time she came to meet him in Pretoria Central. They set a date, and Jonathan asked Chrissie to collect his identity book from his mom so that he could use it to enroll in a course. The day before she was due to visit Jonathan for the first time, she met Jonathan's mother.

"She was delighted to meet me," Chrissie says. "She asked if I knew what Jonathan looked like."

When Chrissie told Jonathan's mother she didn't know what Jonathan looked like, but thought he must be good looking like his brother, Jonathan's mother showed Chrissie a picture of him.

"I couldn't believe my eyes," she says. "He was so handsome: muscular, tattooed…" She told Jonathan's mom, "That's definitely my taste in man!"

The day of Chrissie and Jonathan meeting dawned, and Chrissie dressed with care.

"I chose a tight grey and black striped dress and a denim bunny jacket," she says. "I was slim and tanned, and my hair was long. I looked stunning!"

Chrissie had asked two of her closest, longest-standing friends to escort her to the prison, and the trio set off up the busy N3 in a northerly direction. The conversation in the car was excited, Chrissie spoke of her expectations, her fears, her hopes. They giggled nervously throughout the journey.

Arriving at the prison, Chrissie left her two friends waiting for her in the hot Pretoria sun and went alone to meet the man who had occupied so much of her thoughts and time for the last few weeks.

"I was excited," she tells me. "And confident. But also nervous. My emotions were all over the place."

Chrissie had not yet told her parents or her sister about Jonathan. She knew she had to keep her visit to him in prison on the low, imagining all kinds of wild scenarios should they find out she'd been speaking to a convicted murderer, and was now visiting a prison to meet him. Her head was filled with "what ifs" as she entered the facility. *What if I'm not prepared for what's in store? What if I'm in love? What if he breaks my heart?* She reminded herself she could just call it off if Jonathan broke her heart.

"I've always been a live-on-the-edge, with your heart kind of girl," she says.

"Whichever way it went, I knew this was going to be a game-changer," Chrissie reminisces. "I knew it was going to be extraordinary."

Finally emerging from the last security check and entering the prison, Chrissie's first impression was of a pleasant environment. There were dozens of inmates in orange overalls filling the space, sitting and standing, hugging their visitors. People were talking and crying and laughing.

"It wasn't as dark and gloomy as I had expected," she says.

I ask her if she was scared, and she says she wasn't.

"There were plenty of wardens walking around. It's not like the movies," she adds.

It was nothing like *Shawshank Redemption* or *Escape from Alcatraz* – I checked with her.

Chrissie had barely sat down when the man she was there to see walked in smiling broadly. He hugged her – "It felt like it lasted forever!" she says – and took her hand as they sat.

"I immediately felt comfortable."

A friend of Jonathan's had got a small promise ring for him to give Chrissie. Jonathan hadn't known what a promise ring was, but he was thankful. While they were chatting, Jonathan told Chrissie that he had this promise ring for her, and that it symbolised his commitment to her.

"I told her that she was the answer to my prayers."

Promising anything at this stage was a bridge too far for Chrissie, though.

"It felt too much, too soon," she admits. "I told Jonathan I couldn't promise him anything yet."

Jonathan seemed upset ("I was disappointed," he says), so Chrissie told him, "If I ever promise to make a commitment, I will keep it and be unwavering in my support of you."

"Whatever I decided to do," Chrissie would tell me in 2020, "I knew it was going to be a long, hard walk with him. I was already preparing myself for something serious."

Back in Pretoria Central, Jonathan told Chrissie that he understood her.

"But I'm already committed," he said. "I'm ready for this when you are."

He was unwavering in his faith in his vision.

They agreed to keep talking on the phone, and Chrissie said she would come and visit Jonathan. Jonathan gave Chrissie the ring and she put it on.

XV
DISCLOSURE

Chrissie visited Jonathan every weekend.

"Whenever I was in her presence," Jonathan says. "I would go onto a cloud, I'd feel myself drifting. I've never experienced this with someone before. And she felt it too. It would happen, and I would say to her, 'Can you feel, we're going onto the cloud again?' And she would say, 'Yes'."

No affection was allowed in the visiting areas, and Jonathan found that challenging. But, at the end of the visits, he says, "I would walk towards the entrance to go back into the present. I would turn around and see her looking at me. My miracle."

Chrissie slowly started opening up to her friends about Jonathan.

"I was 34 when I met Jonathan," she tells me. "But I hadn't really had any boyfriends. I was dating, sure. But nothing ever serious."

She enjoyed being single and doing as she pleased.

"I came to the conclusion at a young age that if I was going to be in a relationship, the guy must have learnt 'the hard way'. I liked the idea of a bad boy turned good."

Many of Chrissie's friends married young and started families.

"I admired them," she says. "But all I could think of was where the next party was."

Chrissie, instead, travelled the world, worked overseas, partied.

"It was a good life," she says.

"I was quite the rebellious type," she admits. "If I hadn't been chosen to work at Disney World when I was 18, who knows where I could've ended up!"

Some of Chrissie's friends were supportive of her new relationship, some were skeptical. Jonathan and Chrissie both understand others' skepticism.

"They had Chrissie's interests at heart," Jonathan says.

"Some of my friendships became deeper and more intimate after I shared my relationship with Jonathan with friends," Chrissie says. "But I was also surprised that some friendships ended as a result."

Chrissie knew that the next hurdle for her would be to tell her twin about Jonathan. She'd been overhearing Chrissie talking to

Jonathan on the phone every day for weeks, and was threatening to tell their dad that something was going on. Chrissie knew she needed her on their side in the unfolding process of disclosure, but she also knew it wasn't going to be easy.

Chrissie finally plucked up the courage to tell her sister about Jonathan one rainy night while the two of them were out having a good time.

"Sis, I'm desperate to tell you something serious," Chrissie said. "But it's highly confidential. Can I share it with you now?"

"Tell me," Chrissie's twin said, focussing her attention on her.

"You know those phone calls I've been having?" Chrissie's sister nodded. "Well, it's Jonathan Street. We speak often, and I went to visit him the other day."

Chrissie's sister was upset. She left the table and ran outside into the rain. Chrissie followed her and found her crying in the car.

"How can you do this?" she shouted through her tears. "How can you put our family through this?"

"Jonathan has been the best thing that has ever happened to me," Chrissie replied. "Sis, I think it's serious."

Her twin wasn't convinced, but Chrissie pleaded with her.

"Please, Sis. Please come with me to meet him? Come with me to Pretoria Central, then you can judge for yourself.

On the day Chrissie took her sister to meet Jonathan, he was waiting for them in the visiting area. Chrissie wanted to pop into the tuckshop to buy groceries and food for Jonathan, and while she was there, her sister saw Jonathan and decided to play a trick on him. Being Chrissie's identical twin, she approached Jonathan as if she knew him and said, "Hello, my love."

"Obviously, I knew it wasn't Chrissie," Jonathan says. "But it was funny."

It set the tone for the visit, and although Chrissie's sister tried to keep the walls up during the visit, to Chrissie's delight, her sister and Jonathan got on well.

"My sister cried," Chrissie remembers. "She cried during that visit, but when it ended, she said, 'Chrissie, Jonny, look, I'm OK with you guys being with each other. But you have a long, hard walk in front of you.'"

"The best thing about having an identical twin," Chrissie tells me, "is that you share everything."

After meeting Jonathan, Chrissie's sister convinced her that she needed to tell their mother, and together the sisters summoned their mother to a meeting in the 'elephant corner'.

"The elephant corner," Chrissie tells me, "is a place in my parents' home where we like to sit, talk, confide in each other and relax. It's the chill place of the home, the meeting point. It's decorated with elephant paintings and everything to do with elephants.

"By the way," she adds, "the elephant is Jonny's favourite animal."

Chrissie's mother has very strong beliefs. She is an active member of the Church of Jesus Christ of Latter-Day Saints, and the weekend before Chrissie's meeting with her, she'd spoken somewhat prophetically to the congregation of her church about forgiveness.

"It was almost as if this was about to unfold," she says.

Chrissie sat her mom down in the elephant corner and said, "Mom, I'm in love with someone."

Chrissie's mother had always known that the person Chrissie would fall in love with would be different – "Chrissie has unconventional tastes," she says – but this serious approach to the issue made her suspect there was more to what Chrissie was saying.

"Chrissie had sampled most of what life has to offer," she says by way of explanation. "She's very liberal in her outlook."

She'd also suspected that there was something exciting and different happening in Chrissie's life.

"She had such a happy vibe about her – albeit secretive."

Mom prepared herself for what she was about to hear, but Chrissie's story was not at all what she had expected. She let Chrissie finish, and said,

"Chrissie, you're a tough cookie. But this is not going to be easy, not even for you."

"You know," Chrissie's mom confesses to me in 2020. "I was flabbergasted, but I decided just to let it be. I wasn't convinced it would even last."

Relief flooded Chrissie.

"I knew my mom would be right beside me," Chrissie says. "And I knew she and Jonathan would hit it off."

But the doubts still lingered. Chrissie took her mother to meet Jonathan, and remembers standing waiting to enter the visitation area when she started weeping. She took her mom's hand and said,

"Mommy, I'm so sorry. Who does this? Who takes their mother to prison to meet their boyfriend?"

Her mother was sympathetic, though.

"It's OK, my darling," she smiled at Chrissie. "I'm going to speak with him, look into his eyes, and I will know."

"I was nervous!" Chrissie's mom remembers about that visit. "Never in my life have I ever been to a prison, let alone to visit an inmate."

Chrissie settled her mother in the waiting area and went to get drinks for the three of them from the tuckshop. She returned to find her mother and Jonathan holding hands and praying together, tears streaming down both their faces.

"In that moment," she says to me, "I felt so peaceful about it all."

"Jonathan had a rough edge, I could see," Chrissie's mother says of the first time she met him. "But he was groomed and very neat in his prison clothing. He was soft-spoken and sincere, and he was very open and honest answering my questions. He was popular with the other inmates and their families. When I looked at him, I saw a loving and kind gentleman."

Exhausted, driving the opposite direction on the N3, Chrissie put her hand on her mom's thigh and thanked her over and over.

"It's going to be okay, Chrissie," her mother reassured her. "Not everyone gets to love another the way you guys do."

Despite her good feelings about Jonathan, Chrissie's mother wanted her psychologist sister to "check him out."

"I wasn't nervous," Jonathan remembers. "I knew, if I'm transparent, if I'm truthful, if I hide nothing, then I have nothing to fear."

Not only did Chrissie's aunt give her stamp of approval to Jonathan, she adored Jonathan. She also commented on an early draft of this text on invitation from Jonathan, and gave some valuable pointers.

"I was really worried about how my dad would react to the news of my relationship with Jonathan," Chrissie says. I ask her why, and she says, "He's opinionated. He's got a lot to say about people with tattoos."

But now that the rest of the family had met him, she knew it was time to tell him.

"If he'd found out by accident, he would have given me a rough time, even though I was 34 years old!"

With her mom and her twin by her side, Chrissie had courage.

"Dad," she said as they sat at the table. "I'm in love."

"Does he have tattoos?" was his quick reply.

Chrissie knew this would be his first question, so she'd come prepared.

"Mm-hm," Chrissie replied hesitantly, adding, "He's also an inmate at Pretoria Central."

She showed her dad the photo of Jonathan from a recent family day at the prison. In the silence that followed, Chrissie and her twin were nudging each other under the table, waiting for his response and wondering what it would be. Eventually, he spoke.

"I trust he's a good guy?" Chrissie couldn't believe her ears. Her dad went on, "How long does he have left?"

"Five years."

"That's a long time." He shrugged. "But I trust your judgement."

I met Chrissie's dad. He's a typical father of three girls: protective, caring.

"Chrissie's from a 'normal' family," Jonathan tells me. "They're not used to people with a history like mine. She had to deal with all the skepticism from friends and family while I was inside. But she would always turn up and defend me."

He tells me he'd tell Chrissie that she didn't need to defend him to others, that people were justified in passing judgement on his behaviour in the past.

"They're beautiful people," Jonathan says of Chrissie's family. "Meeting them felt so natural and easy."

XVI
CHANGE

"I thought it was impossible," Jonathan says. "I thought I couldn't do it."

He was sitting in his cell, all the work he would need to do to get his matric certificate in front of him.

"I started crying."

Breaking old habits is hard. Jonathan's anxiety at being faced with what was required of him was completely normal, and he puts getting through it down to sheer determination.

"I made a conscious decision," he says. "I would put my head down and complete Grade 12, no matter how long it took."

Jonathan's clever friend from Zonderwater helped him with his studies. By the time he'd completed matric, Jonathan was 35 years old.

"It wasn't just about the certificate," Jonathan tells me. "I realised the determination and perseverance I needed to finish school could be applied to other areas of my life."

Studying made Jonathan aware of the importance of balance in his life, and he decided to pursue business studies.

"It took me double the time of the inmates studying with me to complete, but I didn't let it bother me," he says. "Before, I never finished anything I started. This time, I just wanted to finish what I'd started."

It was during these challenging times that Jonathan began a habit that would see him through.

"When things got tough," he says, "I'd say to myself, 'Jonathan, how bad do you want this? How far will you go to get it?'"

'Resilience' has become something of a buzzword in pop psychology these days, and with good reason. In the time of Covid, new and unforeseen stressors are putting pressure on us all, and the world is needing to forge a new path through unfamiliar territory. I'd define resilience as the positive adaptation to adversity, none of us are born with resilience . But as human beings, we are primed for resilience – it is the characteristic that has allowed for our long history of biological and cultural evolution.

What Jonathan came upon by accident is key: Resilience and balance are connected.

"You know, people used to call me 'punchy' [short for punchdrunk], 'goon', 'the dumb one'," Jonathan says. "That's how they saw me."

I was reminded of a client of mine who nearly came to punches with a colleague who refused to stop calling him 'shorty'. We often unconsciously live out the names we are given by others. For Jonathan, much of his identity was acquired through how he believed he was perceived by people – especially his peers and those he admired. Now he was becoming aware that he needed to change that dynamic if he was to keep from falling back into his old thought and behavioural patterns.

"In prison," Jonathan says, "there is a lot of time to think, to analyse, to learn how to change."

XVII
LEOPARD'S SPOTS

"Aren't you scared of Jonathan?"

I was asked this question so many times during the course of writing this book, by my friends, my family, associates, colleagues, and even sometimes by people I hardly know.

I found the question absurd. The Jonathan I got to know was a man who'd spent most of his adult life behind bars, but not once did I hear him utter a negative word about anyone. I experienced him as open, non-judgemental, empathic and respectful.

But I had to remind myself that Jonathan was not always these things. It took thirteen long years for Jonathan to change. I recalled my sociology lecturer at Rhodes University introducing us to labelling theory in criminology. According to labelling theory, certain attempts to rehabilitate those who have engaged in criminal behaviour can result in the assigning of particular labels, or categories, to those people, for example, 'murderer'. Having been assigned a label, offenders are treated by society on the basis of their labels. With time, labelled individuals internalise and accept their label, leading to the increased likelihood that they will repeat the behaviour that gave rise to the label.

As Daniel Kahnemann so eloquently shows in his brilliant work *Thinking, Fast and Slow*, as a rule, our thoughts, perceptions, beliefs, views and decisions are biased and based on ignorance (if not stupidity). Subsequently, our intuitive thought processes are subject to errors. Human beings, for the most part, are inclined to investigate or problem solve using heuristics, or 'rules of thumb' – a cognitive shortcut that results in simplistic explanations for complex phenomena, frequently riddled with flaws.

My research into compulsions and dependencies over the course of the last two years has reinforced for me that contemporary society is quick to label a problem, express opinion on it and pass judgement, and then to provide an overly simplistic solution to it. At every braai, someone is opining that "corruption is because all politicians are corrupt and they should rot in jail."

I heard the heuristic phrase "a leopard never changes its spots" more than once from people I know while writing this book, occasionally slightly paraphrased as "a criminal will always be a criminal" or "thugs stay thugs" or "once an addict, always an addict".

This attitude on the part of the layman is not only inaccurate, but, if you hold any store by labelling theory, only serves to make real change all the more difficult than it already is.

There were, of course, many factors that contributed to Jonathan's capacity for change – and by extension, the capacity for every individual to change. But chief among them was the belief that change is possible, on Jonathan's part and on the part of the important people in his life.

Part 4:

REDEMPTION

XVIII
RENEWAL

"It's all about perspective," Jonathan tells me. "If you want to feel like a victim and think the world is to blame for your troubles, you will come through the fire as ashes."

Jonathan told me many times in the course of our collaboration that key to his transformation process was to 'renew his mind'. I asked him what he meant by this in an email, and he replied, "We have to fill our minds with new things, new topics, new relationships. We need to change focus and be cognisant of what we talk about, what we think, what we watch. Who are we when no one is looking, when we're alone and nobody knows what we're doing?"

Jonathan came to the conclusion that in those crazy years leading up to his incarceration, his mind was toxic. At the time, he used to blame others for his troubles, but he's come to realise that all our choices are ultimately our own.

"Many people have grown up in squatter camps," Jonathan argues, "surrounded by violence, poverty and substance abuse, and go on to become good people, contributing members of society. I can't blame my circumstances for how I turned out.

"Change starts within."

Having successfully passed matric, Jonathan decided to further his studies and enrolled for an N4 National Diploma in Human Resource Management. He passed with three distinctions, and the official in charge of the prison college asked him if he'd like to facilitate the N4 Entrepreneurship and Business Management programme the next semester.

"I gladly accepted," he tells me. "It was a privilege for me to be able to serve my fellow inmates that way."

The additional responsibility taught Jonathan a lot about time management, especially since he was continuing his own studies at the same time, and enabled him to overcome his fear of speaking in front of people.

"By then," he says, "I'd realised that the only way to beat fear is to face it."

He rose to the challenge, taking care not to overlook anything in the syllabus, and preparing lessons from a variety of textbooks to be sure he didn't pass on outdated information to his students.

"It was so rewarding," he says. "Twenty-three of my students passed, some with distinctions."

Jonathan completed his N6 Certificate in Human Resources Management, and Chrissie attended his graduation ceremony at Leeuwkop Prison.

"It was so amazing to be there!" she says. "The graduating inmates just about brought the rafters down in song. For a few hours, it felt like a conventional graduation ceremony: just normal people doing normal things."

"It was spectacular," Jonathan says. "The professors from UNISA were up on stage in their red, orange and black gowns, there was a choir singing gospel and inspirational songs. For that moment, we were out of prison."

"I felt such pride for those men who were graduating," Chrissie goes on. "Some of them went to prison with little or no education, and they studied under such trying conditions. Can you imagine working so hard so that when you're released you can become an integral part of society? Some of them were even graduating with masters degrees. How wonderful!"

Once a week, schools would visit Pretoria Central Prison as part of the "Pillar to Post" programme, a joint initiative between the Department of Education and the Department of Correctional Services in which learners are introduced to the harsh realities of prison life and educated about the consequences of crime. Jonathan joined the "Pillar to Post" drama group, who were responsible for presenting testimonies, showing learners around the facility, and performing a play for them before engaging in group discussions. The sessions ended with some dance moves to cheer up the saddened hearts of the school kids, and had a significant impact on the visiting pupils and their teachers.

"When I went on trips with the drama group, showcasing "Pillar to Post", Chrissie would be there in the crowd with her tablet, filming."

Jonathan told me often how thankful he is for having Chrissie in his life.

"She has always been there for me. She's proud of me," he says. "Although I was a man on the inside, I had someone who loved me so much."

Chrissie's presence in Jonathan's life seems to have provided him with the motivation to stick to his new course, and the support to confidently grow into his new identity. She was more mature in the relationship, and Jonathan's insecurities didn't seem to threaten her. Thanks to Chrissie, Jonathan discovered that sharing their insecurities and fears brought the two closer, and they built security in one another.

"It helped to make us whole," Jonathan says.

"We've grown spiritually, together," he tells me on another occasion.

During our drives to and from friends and family for our Saturday Sessions, Jonathan's conversation would inevitably return to Chrissie.

"She's my miracle, my godsend."

Jonathan was determined that he would do the right thing by Chrissie.

"All the heartache of the past, all the knowledge gained, needed to be a lesson to me," he says. "Otherwise, what is it all for?"

One Saturday in Pretoria Central's visiting area, Jonathan got down on one knee and asked Chrissie to marry him. To his delight, she said yes, and soon she had "JS" tattooed on her wedding finger as an engagement ring. Chrissie shows me the other tattoos she's had done in tribute to her relationship with Jonathan: A heart on her right index finger and the words "faith love hope" on her forearm. She laughed when I asked her where the commas were in the troika.

"There are no barriers that can stand in the way of love," Jonathan tells me.

XIX
VASBYT

In 2018, Jonathan was moved to another prison nearer his home – hopefully his last place of incarceration. It was difficult for him to move again, he'd made good friends and achieved so much since arriving at Zonderwater in 2014.

"You get into a comfort zone in a prison," he says. "It's hard to change."

Jonathan made a point of highlighting that, during the course of his imprisonment, there had been many good officials who had treated him well and encouraged him. Prison is a tough place. Behind bars, Jonathan says, one needs to be spiritually grounded, and mentally and emotionally strong. Physical fighting doesn't work in there. To survive in prison, Jonathan had to learn to use his mind and control himself.

"It's a volatile place," he says. "It can be calm for months, and seem like a kindergarten. But, in the blink of an eye, all can break loose, then instantly be calm again. There can be violence and death, and then calmness. You never know when this will be repeated."

Jonathan draws a distinction between discipline and punishment. The discipline he acquired through his time in jail may have felt like punishment at times, but he has come to understand it more as a process – and a necessary one at that.

"I needed to look forward into the future, to the end result that will transpire after going through this process."

Change, Jonathan says, comes with sacrifice. It's taxing and difficult. There are painful decisions to be made, and there are times an individual needs to be selfish.

"No one knows us better than ourselves," he says. "What really counts is what happens when no one is looking. We need to look inward and see what needs to change us. Even before the mind, the heart needs to change."

While at the new prison, Jonathan was involved in the personal development programme for offenders called "Heart Work". Chrissie attended the graduation ceremony when the course was complete, where inmates shared their testimonies.

"It was such an emotional day," she says. "I've never cried so much in my life. The themes of forgiveness and change emerged over and over."

Chrissie describes the experience as 'life changing'.

"To be in a room with hardened criminals who have transformed into gentle, soft-spoken, forgiving men, who want to do something with their lives… Prison and their past cannot define them or serve them anymore."

Despite Jonathan's increasing personal awareness and sense of self-efficacy, the lead up to his release from prison was the most difficult time of his entire sentence. The last six months of incarceration seemed to go on forever.

"Everything was difficult and frustrating," he remembers now. "The challenges felt overwhelming."

Jonathan's relationships with family members seemed dire, and he struggled with issues with his fellow inmates.

During this time, Jonathan had another vision.

"I was walking through a sewer," he tells me. "It was big and dirty and had an odour, and I was walking in the dark."

He remembers that he was well-dressed, and walked with perfect posture.

"There was no fear in me, and I knew where I was headed."

After walking for some time, he reached the end of a tunnel and found a staircase leading upwards. Each stair was a piece of iron mounted into the sewer wall. He began to climb the stairs and after some time, a bright white light shone down from above. The light shone brighter as he approached the top.

"It wasn't like the light from the sun," he describes. "It wasn't yellow or orange. This light was white and the brightest light I'd ever seen."

He reached the top of the staircase and found it difficult to get out. He had to squeeze himself through small narrow spaces, but with effort, he finally popped out.

"I looked down," Jonathan says. "And saw that my legs were chained together around the ankles and the chains were hampering me."

An arm appeared and handed him a hacksaw.

"I knew this hacksaw was given to me by my Father, my heavenly Father."

He took the saw and began cutting at the chain. It took some time, but eventually the chain broke and the vision went away.

"God has given us all the tools we need to break our chains," Jonathan tells me about his vision. "He gives us the tools, and we need to use the tools. God didn't cut the chains for me. He gave me the hacksaw to cut my own chains."

XX
GETTING OUT

The day of Jonathan's release finally dawned. All that remained of his in the cell were some toiletries and the outfit he was planning to wear, all his other belongings he'd given away. He'd had his hair cut, and laid out a pair of dark blue chinos, a brown belt, a light blue patterned formal shirt and brown shoes – the clothes Chrissie had bought him for his first graduation. He'd tried to sleep early the night before, but his mind was racing with excitement. He lay on his bed, gazing up, counting the hours.

"I knew I was ready for my future," he says.

"How did you know?" I ask him.

"God prepared me for this point in my life onwards. I was ready, ages ago, in my heart and soul... I don't have the vocabulary to explain it."

At last, morning arrived, and Jonathan had a cold shower before dressing in his civilian clothes. An hour still remained before unlocking, and Jonathan remembers leaning against a wall, waiting, for what seemed like an eternity. A couple of inmates popped by to say goodbye. Some of the brothers in the cell had been happy for him, others not so much. He knew that there may have been jealousy festering in the hearts of some inmates, but their time would come too.

"I was sad for them."

I had often found myself wondering whether this work was morally justifiable. I celebrate Jonathan's rebirth and the implications his transformation has for myself, and for you, and for all of us. But we cannot escape the fact that it came at the expense of the life of another. Is the exchange worth it in utilitarian terms? Change – in both its intention and process – must be morally justifiable.

Another question I have asked myself countless times is, "Was justice adequately served?" Are Jonathan's thirteen years in prison and stringent parole conditions sufficient to consider his dues paid?

I'm reminded that incarceration is meant to correct the mistakes of the past. The Department of Correctional Services is no longer named the Department of Prisons, and the psychology of the name is relevant in this instance. Correctional Services and the systems and structures within which it works are in place to ensure that a fair and just society can function and flourish. The individual's change within this context highlights our obligations towards the collective: Change programmes are as much about building communities as they are about empowering individuals.

Extending this argument, a change-oriented, communitarian community permits a greater degree of liberty and personal freedoms. This is a psychologically safer environment than one driven by fear of punishment and humiliation, and psychological safety facilitates progress, change and growth.

"Walking out of prison felt so unreal," Jonathan says in 2020. "I thought I was in a dream. To meet Chrissie as a free man, to hug and kiss her and to see the joy on her face… it was mind altering."

Jonathan was released on Valentine's Day 2020. Chrissie and three of Jonathan's friends met him at the Correctional Services offices.

"Those people supported me throughout my incarceration," Jonathan says. "They still play a monumental role in my life."

After receiving his parole conditions and completing the paperwork, they headed home.

A crowd of people were waiting at the house to welcome Jonathan, and he was overwhelmed by the feelings of affection, love and warmth.

"It was unlike anything I'd ever experienced before."

Chrissie and Jonathan were married in the garden that same day, surrounded by well-wishers.

"It was a precious, unforgettable day," Jonathan says. "It felt so natural."

Jonathan fell asleep that night with a sense that he was dreaming and would wake from it shortly.

XXI
ON THE OUTSIDE

By the time I met Jonathan, he'd been a free man for four months. He was working with his new wife, Chrissie, and navigating the challenges of returning to civilian life.

"Things have changed so much," he tells me. "There are new building developments, the roads have changed, technology, the cost of living…"

I ask him what it was like to be released into the time of the COVID-19 pandemic, straight into another kind of lockdown, and he answers,

"It still feels like heaven."

Life, he says, is different once things have been taken away. He's grateful to have been granted the opportunity to live a normal life again.

"I know how precious life is now," he says. "The small things… they're actually the big things."

Occasionally, these days, when Jonathan experiences bliss, he reminds himself of how he's hurt others.

"Those places in my life were so dark," he tells me. "I strive to be a better man everyday, to grow spiritually."

"I love you, Mama Bear."

"I love you too, Jonny Bear."

This was how I first heard Jonathan and his mother-in-law speak to each other on the day I met Chrissie's mom.

"If I'd had a crystal ball six years ago," Mama Bear says, "Would I have guessed that Jonny and I would be saying these words to each other today? Twenty-fourteen was the year my mother died, but it was also the year of the birth of this wonderful love affair between two very special people."

In mid-summer of 2020, Jonathan and Chrissie welcomed their daughter into the world. I have a picture Chrissie took of Jonathan and me holding the baby: Two fairly big boys – one tattooed all over, the other cleanskin – a beautiful little girl between us sporting a pink bow in her mop of blonde hair.

I spent many evenings and afternoons with Jonathan and Chrissie throughout the development of this book. Like any newly-wed couple, they'd address each other with terms of endearment, interact playfully. I was struck by the gentle tones they spoke to each other in, how they went out of their way to accommodate each other's needs. But the thing that really stood out for me was how they looked at one another. They always, always made eye contact. It took just two meetings with them to know that they each had only one priority: to the other.

There were times when I observed disagreements between Chrissie and Jonathan, but even then, there was nothing but good intent. I noticed how they actively listened to each other, and often thought that they'd make effective crisis counsellors, such is their talent at listening without judgement. I remember thinking that it seemed as if they'd been together for decades, even though they'd only been living and working together for a few months at the time.

As I was finishing the final draft of this book, I asked Jonathan what has struck him most about life on the outside.

"Even over a year out of prison," he says, "I'm still in awe of how everything's panned out. I never would have dreamed that my life would take this course. I have a beautiful wife I adore, a baby girl who is a gift, a wonderful and supportive family, a career that is blossoming, I'm training and fit, and I have many projects on the go.

"I'm grateful beyond belief."

Change, for Jonathan, was a matter of life and death. Two of his friends observed in interviews that Jonathan would not have survived if it weren't for prison, but there's more to it than that. South Africa's rate of recidivism, or the rate at which convicted criminals reoffend, is exceptionally high, estimated by Professor Marelize Schoeman (Criminology & Security Science, UNISA) to be between 55% and 95%. In other words, around seven in ten ex-cons revert to criminal behaviour following their release from prison.

In my work on compulsions and dependencies, the fact that many people relapse when trying to remain clean and sober demonstrates how hard it is to make change 'stick'. My experience of adult change is filled with mixed messages: I've known alcoholics who have relapsed after decades of sobriety, I've counselled countless athletes who've sworn off partying the night before the big game for years, only to get smashed the night before an all-important final. I've seen organisations pay millions for change and reinvention programmes, only for those inside the business to claim, "the more things change, the more they stay the same."

I have been asked repeatedly, "Will Jonathan stay as he is now?" The less generous boldly claimed, "Jonathan will go back to his old ways and you'll be left the fool." I confess, I've wondered myself if Jonathan will relapse. Will the self-centredness and aggression return, will that switch flick once more?

The clinical and evidenced-based answer is... maybe. Adults fall off the change wagon when day-to-day pressures and anxieties intensify. When daily routines and learnt actions fail, or when support systems disappear, we tend to revert to earlier, more familiar ways of being-in-the-world.

Partly, it is our understanding of change that is at fault. When change is viewed as a checklist of deliverables or activities to be completed, rather than the deep, ongoing internal work that defines endemic change, the result is almost certain to be a reversion to old behaviours.

I doubt that the man I got to know will fall back on his earlier behaviours. Not once did I experience Jonathan playing victim, he consistently owned up to his actions and faults, and he has actively worked on forgiveness and redemption. He displays none of the characteristics of a serial criminal. He's living a virtuous and rewarding life.

As much as I had wanted, all those years ago, to understand the events and circumstances that led to Jonathan's life spiralling out of control, I became increasingly preoccupied by a new question: Why is it that Jonathan Street was capable of the incredible transformation he has undeniably undergone?

Documentary maker and author Polly Morland writes in *The Guardian*, "Real-world stories can make a real-world difference. Change is hard because it is difficult to imagine. And if it is hard to imagine, then it is even harder to do."[1]

The fact of Jonathan's transformation provides proof that real, deep-seated change is possible. But I've never doubted

---

[1] Morland, P. (2016). Is grit something you can learn? The Guardian [online]. Available from: https://www.theguardian.com/commentisfree/2016/may/26/grit-changing -resilience-courage [accessed 25 May 2021].

that. No, for me, Jonathan's story is more of a call to action. The extremes of Jonathan's transformation, the challenges he had to overcome, the hardships he had to endure in the course of his being forged by fire, demonstrate the potential for change in all of us. Yes, change is hard, but it is possible.

The chief reason I invested a year in the narration, research and production of the Jonathan Street story is because it's a clear case of adult change. As imperfect humans, we have so much to learn from cases such as this one.

My work on *Through the Fire* took place at an inflection point in my life. My business was undergoing reinvention, I began a challenging personal change process. I moved homes, experienced new relationships, learnt that I could love again after decades of singularity. Despite my 25 years working with individuals, groups and organisations in their change, transformation and turnaround endeavours, change is still 'at me'.

As the work progressed, I began to see how I may have incarcerated myself in my head: locking myself away and not realising opportunities as I could have. The analytical part of my psyche became joined with the systemic parts, and I discovered that change is more about synthesis than I had imagined. It became clear that world, societal and group processes become individual processes – it seems obvious to me now, but it wasn't at the outset.

Change is both inevitable and deeply unsettling. In our attempts to find security, we tend to cling to what is fundamentally transient, when the more valuable lesson is perhaps to become more skilled at navigating change. Jonathan would frequently say to me, "Just flow, brother." I'm in mid-life, a specialist in change, and only now learning to let the process unfold.

My hope is that Jonathan's story encourages us all to hope for a better future.

One evening, as we made our way home from one of our Saturday Sessions with friends from years gone by, Jonathan said to me,

"Garrath, I have nothing. But I have everything."

XXII
THROUGH THE FIRE

Perhaps the most challenging aspect of life as we tally up eighteen months and counting of living in a global pandemic, is the ongoing sense of uncertainty. The changes the world population has experienced – globally, nationally, in our communities and families, and as individuals – as a result of COVID-19 and the lockdowns and restrictions that came in the virus's wake, are unmatched in recent history. The future is impossible to predict, and circumstances change with breathtaking speed.

When I came home from the jungles of Africa in the early days of the pandemic, I was 'all changed out'. I was exhausted from the change work that I'd been doing, emotionally drained. I had lost enthusiasm for the work I do, and I had become downright cynical about change in all its forms. Embarking on this work had partly been a means for me to take stock of where I was and answer the question that was becoming increasingly hard to ignore: Did I still want to do what I do?

But as the work progressed, I found my enthusiasm for change work returned. And grew.

Part of what makes change so hard is its paradoxical nature: As human beings we are programmed for change. But change frequently comes with unpleasant sensations such as fear, insecurity, loss of control, and we know from experience that change requires hard work, sacrifice, loss. Evolutionarily speaking, repeating behaviour that brings pleasure and avoiding behaviour that brings pain is a survival imperative – that's why it's easier to resist change than to accept it.

Our species enjoys the benefit of a cortex and higher cortical functioning. We have the latitude and longitude of choice: the ability to choose or not to choose, to change or not to change. Sometimes, though, choosing not to change is choosing death: In Jonathan's case, the choice was literal; in most cases, the choice is figurative. Choosing not to change is choosing the death of our personal potential, it's choosing stability and familiarity over growth and self-mastery.

Adding to the complexity of change is the fact of change's constancy: We may choose not to change, but change will happen despite. "No man ever steps in the same river twice," Heraclitus wrote two and half millennia ago. "For it's not the same river and he's not the same man." The world moves on, our species continues to evolve, the people around us change. We may lose our jobs, win the lottery, or find ourselves having to navigate a global pandemic. Change, then, is both a choice and inevitable.

My vision of change begins with three fundamentals. First, the observable evidence of change, in other words, a change in actions and behaviours, tells only part of the story. What can be seen is the result of deeper and more powerful emotional drivers and forces. Our emotional universe accounts for most of our behaviours.

Second, genuine, deep personal change almost always takes place through the advent of a personal crisis. This type of crisis hits you at the core of your being: It is a crisis of loss, and it comes with the weight of potential consequences. It shakes your values and purpose, and it is deeply felt.

Third, the process of change often results in what seems like ridiculous behaviour. I've witnessed adults panic, freeze or fight when confronted with change. Even when the promise of change may be overwhelmingly positive, individuals may withdraw, become aggressive, experience anger or depression. Emotional reactions to the prospect of change are unpredictable, iterative and non-linear. It's a confusing time, but it's helpful to remember the psychoanalytic view that behind every irrationality runs a rationality. While the behaviour may appear strange or out of character, there is a perfectly logical explanation for it. If you're familiar with the work of Elisabeth Kübler-Ross, her theory of the five stages of grief is relevant here: People in the midst of change experience denial, anger, bargaining, depression, and finally acceptance – sometimes in the course of a day or even a few hours.

These three features of change highlight for me the fact that change is an emotional process. Change interventions, whether personally driven or expertly facilitated, need to be orchestrated from the emotional centre.

Perhaps one of the most difficult aspects of Jonathan's transformation was the development of his affective and emotional world. Jonathan's ability to centre in on the emotional stance of the people he encountered was one of the personality traits I first observed in him. But this skill was hard-earned. First, he had to learn how to identify his own feelings, then how to process them in an effective way. Once he could recognise, name and process his own feelings, he was able to appreciate where others are at emotionally, providing him with deeper and more significant insight into others.

The reward of this emotional competency was that Jonathan was empowered to connect with others in a more authentic way. As a result, relationships took a different turn while he was in prison. I remembered Jonathan telling me how his heart had been broken so many times in prison, suggesting he is a sensitive and caring soul. Part of his change required him to read people better, learn to protect himself from hurt, and draw healthy boundaries.

The entrance of Chrissie in Jonathan's life coaxed Jonathan to lower the unhealthy boundaries he'd developed earlier in his life in response to negative circumstances, and her love, support and commitment restored Jonathan's faith in others. Authentic relationships became central to him.

These positive changes in Jonathan's emotional life gave him the confidence to stop masking. Masking is the concealing of your natural personality to conform to social pressures. Jonathan's aggression masked his inner turmoil, his anger hid his fear. Jonathan hid his insecurities behind bling, numbed his feelings of isolation with drugs and alcohol. His tattoos fed both his need to be noticed, and his inner emptiness.

It's interesting to talk about masks in the context of Covid: I've observed that it has become even more difficult to get to know the 'real' person behind the mask these days, both the Covid-enforced mask and the figurative mask we wear to present ourselves to the world. My one-on-one work with people in authority frequently includes lowering the masks they wear so that they can be more authentic, trustworthy and human.

Jonathan had to learn that the bravado-filled, pseudo-dominance charade he had played for most of his life was in large part responsible for the tragedy that unfolded. Once he replaced his masks with transparency and vulnerability, his personal change could begin.

These three emotional aspects of adult transformation: emotional intelligence, authentic relationships and transparency, are key to developing self-awareness. Self-awareness is a building block of adult transformation. But Jonathan's change didn't begin there.

The day Jonathan was called to his faith, when he was drawn to the Bible study group in that cell in Sun City, is the day Jonathan found his purpose. Prior to that, Jonathan found no meaning in his life. Jonathan's faith provided the ballast for his personal change programme.

As much as our purpose gives our life substance, it also provides direction. Jonathan's faith provided him with the necessary guidance to remodel his values based on scripture.

Jonathan's purpose is also the reason he began to think differently, firstly about himself and later about others.

"I stopped thinking the angry and horrible thoughts," I remember him telling me. "I started seeing the good in me and others. It was central to my changing."

Before long, these thoughts became constructive actions. Jonathan adopted a routine and rhythm that became his new 'way of working'. He woke early, was first in the showers, trained, read the scriptures. He was present for group work and inner work, engaged with others about redemption and change. This regular repetition of healthy behaviours, filling his time with beneficial activities, instilled discipline in Jonathan and enhanced his physical and emotional well-being.

In turn, Jonathan's routine allowed him to develop further skills and competencies that helped to increase his confidence. Finishing matric demonstrated to Jonathan the benefits of balance and commitment, and spurred him on to study further. Teaching, preaching and being involved in the drama group provided him with concrete skills such as creative expression, time management, self-care and self-management skills, while taking care of his psychological, mental and spiritual self.

Hope emerged consistently in this work, as a theme, a concept, a practice and a philosophy. I will never forget Jonathan's story of the day he was convicted to 24 years in jail. He was 27 years of age, hungover, sitting in the back of a police van being taken to prison. He estimated that he may be released close to his fiftieth birthday. He had nothing, he was completely alone. In that moment, Jonathan was hopeless.

Now, 14 years later, Jonathan is free. He is married, starting a new career, fit and healthy, and a new father.

"Hope," Jonathan says, "was all I needed to get the process started."

Change was only possible when Jonathan believed there was a future for him, that he could reach his potential, that his incarceration was a temporary situation. Jonathan had to believe that he could be transformed, and that he could redeem himself and be forgiven.

Hope is not an emotion, but a state of mind. It is a verb: it is active, not passive. Hope is not merely optimism, or the expectation that "things will be OK", because the act of hope encompasses the vision of a better future and an inclination to find a pathway to it. Hope is what gives us the strength to persevere, even when all seems lost.

My immediate reaction to the first conversation I had with Chrissie, the encounter that sparked the chain of events that has culminated in this work, was hope. Jonathan's story is a story of hope: Hope for redemption, for a second chance, for forgiveness. Hope in the potential of adult transformation.

This is a powerful and positive message during a time of pessimism, little confidence, sagging hope, sadness, loneliness, fear, anxiety and depression. The Jonathan Street story provides an antidote to the narrative of doom and gloom that fills so much of our public discourse.

As I wrote and rewrote this work, getting to know Jonathan, grappling with my own transformations, and coming to grips with a changed world, I become deeply appreciative of the opportunity it brought me to revisit my theory of personal change, to refine my thinking on the subject, and to add to my approach to change.

Jonathan's story reinforced many of my assertions about change. It confirmed for me that change happens in conjunction with a crisis of loss, that it is accompanied by conflict of some kind, and that it requires us to confront ourselves. I was reminded that change will be met with resistance, that it is frequently avoided – sometimes for life. It highlighted the necessity of support structures as we work through the process of change. It deepened my understanding of change as primarily an emotion, that it elicits various psychological processes, and that it can result in behaviour that seems irrational.

Change requires the skills to initiate and facilitate change. These need to be deliberately identified and consciously developed. Undergoing change requires the support of others – attempting deep-seated change by 'white knuckling' it alone is difficult.

But the year-long exercise of documenting Jonathan's transformation also brought up a number of tensions, which has led to my theory *moving*. Talking about the project with others inevitably elicited a response along the lines of, "You seem to have been deeply affected by the story," and they were right. Jonathan's story is a *moving* one, and I was *moved* by it. I was *moved* by Jonathan's transformation, his new belief and values, his care and love for others.

In reflecting on the work we did together, Jonathan says,

"I was deeply affected by the opportunity to examine myself and my past. Working with you has propelled me to a new sphere, a future my mind did not fathom before I met you."

I'm thankful that Jonathan has found value in our collaboration, and privileged to have played a small part in his reintegration into society. But just as he gained much from this process, so did I.

My Jonathan Street experience got me *moving*. Writing this book saw me *moving* to different and exciting places: in my head, in my heart, in my current and future relationships and friendships, in my business, in my values, assumptions and values, and in my endeavours. It got me *moving* towards the people, things and places that make me feel alive and excited. It allowed me to exit those that hindered *movement*. I realised that some of the relationships I had been part of for decades didn't permit or allow movement, rather having the opposite effect and keeping the toxicity in place. I had to draw a boundary, confront what and who I needed to, so that I could *move along*.

My theory of personal change *moved* because I opened myself to *moving*… in all its glory. My affective and emotional self experienced *movement* to a different place, one that I had not expected or planned – it simply 'flowed', to use Jonathan's word.

The theme of *moving* became central to 2020 and 2021 for me. While editing this work, I decided with the help of a close and wonderful colleague that I'm going to keep *moving* – on all levels. *Movement*, I sense, will become a permanent fixture.

Jonathan's story of his journey through the fire of transformation to redemption has enabled me to articulate my theory of personal change – a complex, contradictory and nuanced process – with a simplicity and clarity I've never achieved before.

Adult transformation is primarily an emotional process. The building blocks of adult transformation are purpose, self-awareness, daily action, and hope. Change enables us to find freedom in confinement.

And this is the payoff of change: I'm excited by and hopeful for what tomorrow holds. Like Cortez on the shores of the New World, I have burnt the ship I arrived on, because this is home and there's no going back.

Acknowledgements

Garrath would like to thank Jonathan and Chrissie for letting him enter their lives, their home, families and friends. Without them, this remarkable story would not have been told.

Jonathan would like to thank many friends and family who supported him before, during and after "Going through the Fire".

Jesus
Department of Correctional Services
Garrath
Khalil
Charlene
Christine
Vaughn
Michelle
Alan
Greg
Gorette
Des
Betsie
Ferdie
Lorraine
Matthew
Chrissie
Hari
Dianne
Liz
Heleni - Jean
Ellie
Kevo
Nik
Ja
Clivey
Jared
Lee
Jax
Mon
Dave
Priscilla
Matt

Brendon (my MMA coach)
Manie
Gaylin
Val
Jc
Byron
Shannon
Pauly
Graeme
Natalie
Gert
Sarita
Jimmy
Reinach
Nix
Darrell
Brate
Maudie
Quinzell
Vundla
Gareth
Mikhalia
Tina
John
Richi
Arturo
Jan
Candy
Rachel
Denise
Simone
Katie
Angie
Links
Pippa
Philipa
Shelly
Jason
Danielle
Clint
Clonari

Rob
Darren
Deon
Jacques
Telford
Dono
Keith
Gaye
Stanley
Koper
Johan
Daan
Lente
Tinus
Virgil
Dean
Devon
Tv
Grant
Stel
David
Erica
Michele
Linda
Musa
Adam
Marc
Tshidi
Jennifer
Stephen
Liz
Elias
Dotty
Carol
Heinz
Lynn
Miguel
Mitch
Emily
Phillip
Khosi

Crystal
Sonet
Phrosné
Inez
Susan
Erin
Landon
Priya
Justin
Tshepiso
Vuyo
Rudie
Fifi
Leon
Kelly
Sharamunti
Clive
Jizo
Priscilla
Dinx
Daléne
Vanessa
Dino
Jaco
Ruta
Aric
Giannis
Gary
Donna
Justin
Leslyn
Debra
Gielie
Mike
Tośa
Lionel
Warren
Lauren
Greg
Nomsa

Thanks

www.ingramcontent.com/pod-product-compliance
Lightning Source LLC
Chambersburg PA
CBHW062103270326
41931CB00013B/3199